SKIPPY'S FAMILY

other books
by STEPHEN W. MEADER

THE BLACK BUCCANEER
DOWN THE BIG RIVER
LONGSHANKS
RED HORSE HILL
AWAY TO SEA
KING OF THE HILLS
LUMBERJACK
THE WILL TO WIN
WHO RIDES IN THE DARK?
T-MODEL TOMMY
BAT
BOY WITH A PACK
CLEAR FOR ACTION!
BLUEBERRY MOUNTAIN
SHADOW IN THE PINES
THE SEA SNAKE
THE LONG TRAINS ROLL

SKIPPY'S FAMILY

STEPHEN W. MEADER

ILLUSTRATED BY ELIZABETH P. KORN

SOUTHERN SKIES

© 1945 HARCOURT, BRACE AND COMPANY, INC.
© 2006 SOUTHERN SKIES LLC

All rights reserved

ISBN 978-1-931177- 68-9 cloth
ISBN 978-1-931177- 69-6 paperback

SOUTHERN SKIES

LITTLE ROCK, ARKANSAS
www.southernskies.com

Dedication

The republication of this book is dedicated with love to Wayne Freppon---world's best brother-in-law, coach, educator, dog lover, loyal and trusted friend of 45 years---by Jerry Atchley

Skippy's Family

FOREWORD

This is the true history of a small, brown mongrel dog, a wholly unremarkable dog except to the family which knew him best. For seventeen years he was a full-fledged member of that family—as definite a personality as Dad or Mother or any of the four children. He shared our ups and downs, our tribulations and our holiday moods.

He was sometimes comical, sometimes exasperating, but always intelligent, lovable, loyal and courageous. His firmness of purpose was a household byword.

When, in the fullness of years, the time for parting came, it was a black day for all of us. We miss him still, though many months have passed. But he left with us a host of whimsical recollections, some of which I have set down in this story of his life.

Being adopted by a dog is a serious matter and should not be entered into lightly. Like marriage, it is a relationship that depends for its success on patience and understanding. Sometimes it involves the possibility of heartbreak. Yet the human being who has never known the companionship and devotion of a dog has surely missed a worth-while part of living.

STEPHEN W. MEADER

SKIPPY'S FAMILY

ONE

IT was six o'clock on one of those miserable winter evenings that sometimes come between Thanksgiving and Christmas. Snow had fallen the night before and through the morning, but at midday it had turned to a bleak, soaking drizzle of rain. Slush lay deep in the gutters, and the cars that churned along Main Street threw geysers of muddy water from their tires. The street lights had been on for hours when Dad got off the bus. Coat collar up and dripping hat brim pulled down, he waded across to the curb and started up the front walk to the house.

As usual there were three small heads in the lighted window of the living room. But tonight, instead of bobbing down and racing to the front door, they stayed there, curiously quiet.

"Perhaps," Dad thought, "they didn't see me—it's so dark and rainy." He clumped up the porch steps, stamping to

Skippy's Family

shake the slush off his rubbers. And as he reached for the doorknob he gave a start. There at his feet, below the threshold, lay something dark and wet and shaking—something that whimpered faintly.

"What the—" Dad exclaimed. "Here—get out, you!" He stamped again, threateningly this time, and was about to continue with some general remarks on stray dogs when the door opened a crack. In the panel of light, three heads appeared. The smooth, dark one belonged to Steve, aged nine. Jane's Dutch bob came next. And in the foreground stood six-year-old John, his solemn, cherubic face topped with a halo of wavy blond hair.

All three looked scared, but desperately hopeful. As Dad might have expected, it was John who had been elected to do the talking.

"Daddy," he piped, "he's a awful nice little dog, an' he's hurt."

Dad looked again at the bedraggled little beast, more clearly visible now in the light from the doorway. The dog scrambled weakly to its feet and made an effort to lick Dad's hand, but he snatched it away quickly.

"Good gosh!" he snorted. "Where'd the filthy little pooch come from? And why did he have to pick *our* front porch, of all places? Probably rabid and certainly mangy. If he doesn't clear out I'll call the police—have him taken to the pound."

John stood his ground, white-faced but undaunted.

Skippy's Family

"Look at him, Daddy. He's a nice little dog—an' pretty—an' he's hurt. His tail's hurt."

Against his will, Dad bent over for a closer look. The patch at the base of the tail that he had taken for mange was a raw, bleeding bruise. He stood up again, hesitating, and Steve spoke up.

"All we want, Daddy, is to give him sump'n to eat an' put some vaseline on him an' let him sleep down cellar. Just this one night—he's so cold an' wet."

"That's right, Daddy," Jane put in. "Just tonight is all. Mother said it's all right—if you said we could."

"Well," Dad replied. "We'll talk about it. I don't think Mother *does* want him in the house—even down cellar. But right now we've got to go in and shut that door before you all freeze to death. No, John—he'll have to stay out here. Maybe he'll go away and leave us in peace."

Dad took off his wet hat, overcoat and rubbers and put them in the closet. Mother was in the kitchen, taking supper off the stove and supervising the table manners of ten-months-old Peggy Lu, who sat in her high chair, gurgling and splashing strained vegetables with her bunny spoon. Mother's look, as she lifted her face to be kissed, was half harassed, half amused. When she spoke it was not of dogs.

"Pretty awful out, isn't it, dear? Hadn't you better change those wet trousers and socks and shoes?"

"I'm all right," Dad fumed. "Look here—what about this stray pup out on the porch? You don't want fleas in the house, do you? Or smelly, wet dog hairs?"

"No," Mother admitted calmly. "But I hate to disappoint the children. I'm afraid they'd cry all night. After all, they're just being kindhearted. When you think of the bad, mischievous things they do, I don't believe we should discourage any signs of goodness."

Dad opened his mouth to speak, then shut it again. In some amazement he watched small Jane set the table in the dining room without being urged. Steve asked him politely if he would like his slippers brought from upstairs. John sat on a footstool in the corner and stared straight ahead, a far-off, dreamy look in his wide blue eyes.

The tension was still uncomfortable when they sat down at the table. Dad knew that every ear was cocked toward the front porch, but the only sound he could hear was the

Skippy's Family

beating swish of rain. Ladling out the stew, he tried to be natural and hearty. "Well, kids," he asked jovially, "how did you amuse yourselves, this rainy afternoon?"

The silence was heavy. John raised a forkful of food, then put it back on his plate. "His name," he said, addressing nobody in particular, "is Skippy."

"What's that?" Dad asked. "Whose name?"

"That little dog," John replied. "His name's Skippy, like the little boy in the funnies."

"Look here!" Dad exploded. "Do you mean you know this dog—know who he belongs to? I'll take him right back there after supper."

John's eyes were innocent. He shook his head. "No," he said. "We just saw him today."

"And you don't know where he came from?"

"He came out of the street," said Jane.

"We think he was hit by a car," said Steve.

Mother smiled but did not meet Dad's eye. "He crawled up on the Herrs' porch, next door," she explained. "John was over there paying them a visit."

"And," Jane put in, "he kept saying, 'Missy Herr, can I have him? Missy Herr, can I have him?'"

Dad frowned. "So," he said accusingly, "you dragged him over here, did you, John?"

"No," the little boy replied. "I just came home an' he came too."

"What I'd like to know," said Dad, "is how you found

out his name. Is it on his collar?"

"He hasn't got any collar," Steve answered. "But we know his name's Skippy 'cause John called him that an' he tried to wag his tail, only he couldn't wag very well 'cause he was hurt."

Dad pushed back his chair and stalked purposefully to the telephone in the front hall. "Give me the police," he told the operator. "Hello—that you, Chief? Look, there's a stray dog on our front porch. Little, brown, long-haired pooch. No—no breed that I ever saw. Just a mongrel. Anybody reported losing a dog? Well, if you hear of one being lost, let me know. We'll be glad to get rid of him."

The stricken faces of the three children stopped him in his tracks at the dining room door. "Oh, come now," he said, in an effort to be cheerful. "Let's all eat our supper. That's mighty good stew."

"We aren't very hungry," Jane murmured.

"We're saving it," said Steve.

"For Skippy," said John.

Dad caught Mother's warning look, and sat down in red-faced silence. When the unhappy meal was over at last, and Jane started helping Mother clear away the dishes, Dad called the boys.

"All right," he said, "we'll take a look at him. But I don't want to get my clothes dirty. Where's that old coat I wear to carry out ashes?"

John had opened the front door. "He's still here, Daddy,"

Skippy's Family

he reported.

"Yes," said Dad. "I was afraid of that."

He stooped gingerly and picked up the trembling animal in his arms. "You shut the front door, John," he commanded. "And, Steve, go ahead and turn on the cellar light. We'll take him right down there."

The dog was still trembling when Dad deposited him on a newspaper on the cellar floor. In the bright light from the bulb over the washtubs, all the stray's pitiful thinness and dirtiness were revealed. He was about the size of a beagle hound but the hair of his coat, over the protruding ribs, was as long as a collie's. It clung to him now, wet, muddy and matted with cockleburs. He looked, as Dad muttered to himself, like an oversized drowned rat. But there was one thing about this dog that Dad had not counted on. It was the expression in his eyes. They gazed upward now, soft and brown and beseeching, and Dad was taken off his guard.

"Why, you poor little cuss," he said huskily, and the dog's bedraggled tail moved in a feeble arc.

"Steve," said Dad, "run up and ask Mother if she's got an old turkish towel. We're going to give this feller a bath."

The little mongrel made no fuss when they put him in the laundry tub. Dad scrubbed his hide with warm water and soap, pulled out the burs, rinsed him well and rubbed him down with the big towel. The injury on the top of the tail, close to the body, looked like a deep cut of some kind. It had laid bare the bone but apparently the tail itself wasn't broken. The bleeding had stopped.

Steve was ready with the jar of vaseline, and Dad applied it generously to the wound. The dog winced once or twice but made no outcry. He lay there on the paper by the

furnace, where he had been put to dry, and looked at them all with eyes that were trustful and disarming.

"I think," said Dad, "that he's just about starved to death. Wonder if Mother saved any of that beef stew."

Before he had finished speaking, John's chubby legs were hurrying up the stairs. "I'll get it, Daddy," he called breathlessly.

He was gone only a matter of seconds. When he reappeared he had a tin pie plate heaped with food. Close behind

Skippy's Family

him came Jane, carrying a bowl of water, and Mother, drying her hands on her apron.

"Just look at him eat," said Mother. "I never saw anything so hungry in my life. Poor little tyke!"

She bent over for a closer look at the famished little stranger and gave an exclamation of surprise. "Why," she said, "he's actually beautiful! His fur's so soft and fluffy and long. He isn't really brown, either. Look at the hair on his tummy and the fringe on his tail. It's buff-colored. Just the outside hairs on his back and sides are black and brown. And the white patch at his throat is like a little shirt front. And those long, silky ears! And his eyes! Did you ever see such eyes?"

Dad grinned. "Now, now," he said, "don't go into ecstasies. He'll never take any ribbons for beauty, but I'll grant he looks a lot better now he's washed. Come on, kids, we'll go upstairs and let him finish his supper. He'll be warm and dry down here, and you can all look at him once more before you go to bed."

They obeyed with a cheerfulness that surprised their father. John, usually rebellious at being packed off ahead of the others, was eager for bedtime tonight. At seven o'clock he pushed his Buddy-L truck into a corner and yawned elaborately. "I want to go to bed now," he announced. "Can I go down cellar first?"

Dad nodded. "Go ahead," he said, "but don't stay long. Remember, the little dog's awfully tired. He wants to sleep

Skippy's Family

now."

They heard his small feet trudge down the stairs and low cooing sounds came from below. After a minute or two he ascended again, and his childish treble piped from the head of the steps. "Good night! Good night, Skippy!"

An hour later the two older children had also paid their respects to the guest in the cellar and gone to bed. When Mother came downstairs from hearing their prayers and tucking them in, she smiled over her knitting.

"I suppose," she said, "there aren't three happier youngsters in America than those, tonight."

"Umph," Dad grunted. "Well, we'll see in the morning. I'm not looking forward to the job of cleaning up the messes that pup is sure to leave downstairs. Besides—I thought you were cured of dogs after the trouble we had with poor Sandy."

Mother nodded. "I thought so too. But Sandy was a pedigreed dog. I've heard somewhere that mongrels are likely to be healthier. Isn't that true?"

"Search me," Dad sighed. "I doubt if they're easier to housebreak, though."

At ten-thirty Dad went down to fix the fire for the night. The little waif looked up from his place by the furnace and watched while coal was shoveled into the firebox and the dampers closed. Dad reached down surreptitiously to pat the round, sleek head and the dog's plumed tail wagged in friendly fashion. The muzzle he touched to Dad's hand was

Skippy's Family

cool and moist.

"No fever, eh?" Dad murmured. "I guess you're going to be all right—Skippy."

He tiptoed into the upstairs bedroom and peeped at the baby, rosily asleep in her crib. As he started to undress, the telephone jangled in the hall below.

"Now who," asked Mother, "can that be, at this time of night?"

She heard Dad's voice, muffled so as not to wake the children. "Hello . . . Who? Oh, yes, Chief. . . . Haven't heard anything, eh? . . . You can take him away in the morning? Well—no, don't bother. Unless somebody claims the pup, I guess we can—sort of take care of him here. Thanks. Good night, Chief."

Mother gave a little contented sigh and snuggled into her pillow. She was still smiling in her sleep when Dad came up to bed.

TWO

IN the cold darkness before dawn Dad was wakened by a sound of whispering and a patter of slippered feet on the stairs. He looked at his watch. Six o'clock—three-quarters of an hour before getting-up time. Nevertheless he hauled himself out of bed and struggled into his bathrobe. As long as he was awake he might as well open up the fire and find out what those rascals were doing.

It wasn't until he reached for the light switch at the top of the cellar stairs and found it already on that he remembered Skippy. Down by the furnace the three children squatted in a blissful huddle. John's small fat arms were around the dog's neck, and Steve and Jane were patting him steadily.

"Gosh," groaned Dad, "I suppose you've got yourselves all dirty. He's sure to have messed the place up."

But a hasty glance around revealed that the basement floor was spotless. He went to the slanting cellar door and opened it. "Come on, Skip," he called. "It's high time you took a run outside."

Skippy's Family

In some dismay the children watched the dog break loose from their embraces and trot across to the door.

"He'll run away," wailed Jane.

"No," said Dad. "He has to go out. You'll find he's still here at breakfast time. Cut along back to bed now."

Mother had turned on the light and was getting up when he returned. "What was the matter?" she inquired sleepily.

"Not a thing," said Dad. Then, somewhat irrelevantly, "That's a remarkable dog—a most surprising dog."

The weather had cleared in the night and the slush was frozen in icy ruts. Coming down to breakfast, Dad found the three older children dressed and in the dining room, their noses pressed to the side window. Looking over their heads he saw Skippy trotting about the yard, nosing at bushes, learning the geography of the place. Already he seemed very much at home.

"It's terr'ble cold," said Steve. "Couldn't we let him in now, Daddy?"

"Not now," Dad replied. "He's enjoying himself, and as long as it doesn't rain, that thick coat of his will keep him fine and warm. Listen, kids—I've decided to let you keep Skippy. That is, unless someone else claims him. But we're going to have definite rules. One is that he's to stay outdoors except nights and in bad weather. Another is that he isn't to be fed between meals. He'll get one good meal in the evening and a couple of dog biscuits in the morning. Mother's going to get some at the store today. If you want him

Skippy's Family

to be healthy and stay with us a long time that's the way he must be fed. Understand?"

The three heads nodded solemnly.

"All right. Now another thing. I know you want to play with him after school. Remember he's been hurt, and don't be rough with him till that sore tail heals up. And keep him away from the street. You don't want him to chase cars or get run over."

"We'll take awful good care of him," Jane promised.

"An' I've got an old busted strap off my roller skate he can have for a collar," Steve added.

"I'm goin' to play with him soon as I get home," beamed John, who was in first grade and had only half a day of school.

When Dad went out to catch his bus, the little dog followed at his heels as far as the curb. "No," said Dad firmly. "Go home now, Skippy." And obediently Skippy returned to the front porch. Looking back from the corner at the bus stop, Dad could see a small, dark dot, still sitting there by the steps.

That evening, as he came up the front walk, Dad was half expecting Skippy to trot out to meet him. When it didn't happen he was first disappointed, then worried. He whistled and called the dog's name.

A faint answering bark came from inside the house. When he opened the door, the little stray was waiting in the hall, pleased and hopeful. Dad said nothing. He just looked down

Skippy's Family

reproachfully, and the dog hung his head. The big brown eyes were full of shame and sadness as Skippy turned and walked toward the kitchen, dejection in every line of his body.

"Now, see here," called Mother, "were you scolding that poor dog? He's not to blame. I called him in myself when I saw him shivering out there after sunset."

Dad grinned as he kissed her. "No," he said. "I didn't scold him. Didn't have to. That pup has a conscience!"

The children had been hiding. Now they popped out from nooks and corners to swarm hilariously over their father.

"Can we have him in the house, Daddy?" they cried. "Can he sleep in my bed?" asked John.

Dad laughed and patted Skippy's round head. "As long as he behaves himself," he answered, "he might as well stay in the house. But we'll give him a bed of his own, if there's an old quilt or something around."

After supper Mother brought a worn and faded quilt down from the attic and Dad folded it and put it in the corner under the kitchen table. Skippy came and sniffed at its invitingly soft surface, then looked up at the circle of faces, hardly daring to believe the bed was intended for him.

"Go ahead, Skip," said Dad. "Lie down. It's all yours." The little dog tested the quilt with a diffident paw, turned around two and a half times, and settled down with a sigh of contentment.

Skippy's Family

"I wish," said John, "I could lie down with him. He looks so comf'able."

* * *

It was amazing what food and warmth and the loving care of the children did for Skippy. He was no longer cringing

or pitiful. Within a week he was as frisky and full of bounce as a rubber dog. The hurt place on his tail healed quickly and the tail itself was held proudly aloft like a banner, its buff plumes waving.

Along with his confidence, he recovered the use of his voice. It was, the family decided, a fairly good baritone—neither shrill and yapping nor hoarsely profundo. And he did not bark without reason.

He had a businesslike, warning bark for such occasions as the arrival of the postman, whom he tolerated in spite of a definite hostility toward uniforms. For chasing sparrows,

Skippy's Family

rabbits and cats, his bark was more staccato, but still gay. When other dogs or strange people passed the house or peddlers came to the door he could put real menace into his barking, and the growl that rumbled in his throat was enough to make a trespasser turn pale.

On the first Monday morning after his arrival the plump colored woman who came to do the washing was greeted at the back door by such a fury of sound that it

took Mother five minutes to persuade her to come in. Once told that this was Susie and he must be nice to her, Skip offered no more objections to her presence. But it was a

Skippy's Family

month before she felt quite at ease with the little dog.

Meanwhile the children discovered new wonders in him every day. He would submit to any amount of petting and mauling without complaint. Coming home one wintry night, Dad was puzzled to see three small figures in snow suits pushing a doll carriage along the walk under the street light. Lying back in the carriage was what looked like a big rag doll, dressed in a baby bonnet.

"What the dickens," asked Dad, "are you imps up to at this time of night?"

"We're giving Skippy an airing," giggled Jane.

"Look at him, Daddy," John urged. "He likes it."

Bending closer, Dad saw the dog reclining on the cushions, his paws folded demurely on his breast. Under the frills of the baby cap his pointed nose twitched humorously and he rolled a sheepish eye upward at Dad, as much as to say, "I know I look silly, but they're having fun."

The little procession moved slowly back toward the house. And all the way—up the walk, up the steps and into the front hall—Skip lay limply on his back, never moving a muscle, his tongue lolling out with the suggestion of a foolish grin. It wasn't until Jane untied the bonnet strings under his chin that he sprang out of the carriage and ran frisking about, trying to lick each of the children's faces in turn.

Peggy Lu, the baby, was too young to share the enthusiasm of her brothers and sister for their new playmate. At first she regarded the dog with a mixture of fear and delight.

Skippy's Family

Crawling around in her pen in the living room, she would crow at Skippy with excited glee and throw her playthings in his direction. But if he came too near she usually beat a hasty retreat.

For his part, Skip was too much of a gentleman to press his attentions on the young lady. He understood from the start that Peggy was a special treasure in the household—someone to be adored and protected.

When she was taking a nap in her coach on the front porch, Skippy would lie quietly by the steps for hours, guarding her slumber. Birds could hop past, a few feet from his nose, without eliciting a single bark. When she was awake, of course, it was a different matter. At such times he made as much noise as he considered necessary in taking care of the place, but he still kept an eye on the perambulator.

Once, when Peggy Lu had been napping on the porch for an hour or more and Mother had gone out to the back yard to hang freshly washed diapers on the line, there was a sudden frenzy of barking. Skip came tearing around the corner of the house, sprang up on Mother, barked sharply, and darted toward the front once more, looking over his shoulder and begging her to follow.

His actions were as plain as words. She dropped her clothespins and ran. When she reached the porch there was Peg, standing up in the coach and joyfully bouncing it on its springs. And one front wheel was teetering in the air,

Skippy's Family

over the edge of the top step. Even though the brake was locked, the baby's jounces had been so vigorous that she had moved the carriage all the way across the porch—a distance of several yards.

Mother grabbed the carriage just as it started to tilt forward. She sat down, breathless, on the steps, and cuddled Peggy Lu close in her arms. For a moment she was so busy soothing her, frightened out of her merry mood by the suddenness of her rescue, that she paid no attention to Skippy. Then his nose nudged her knee and she looked down into his anxious eyes. Tenderly she laid a hand on his head. There was no need to speak. Her smile was enough.

"Little dog," it told him, "you can stop worrying about a home. You've got one with us for as long as you live."

THREE

A FIVE-INCH snowfall came, followed by a crisp, cold, sunshiny Saturday. Aided by the boys and Skip, Dad shoveled out the walks and cleared a drift from the garage door. He used the big wooden snow shovel, of course. Steve struggled manfully with the coal scoop from the cellar, and John got along as best he could with the little tin spade that went with his beach bucket. Skip's efforts were confined to frisking and tearing around the yard, belly deep in the light, dry snow.

"What do you s'pose we'll get for Christmas, Daddy?" Steve asked.

"I want a snow shovel just like yours, only little," said John.

"I don't," said Steve. "I want a Flex'ble Flyer an' a pair o' skis an' a Buddy-L steam shovel an'—an' a pony an' a 'lectric train—an'—"

"Whoa up there!" laughed Dad. "It's only a few days to Christmas now, and I reckon Santa's too busy to get all those things together just for one boy. Remember, he's got a lot

Skippy's Family

of other kids to think about, too. I've seen a good many Christmases and I've found it's more fun to be surprised than to get just the things you think you want."

Steve looked glum and went back to his shoveling. He was pretty sure there was a flaw in Dad's philosophy somewhere, but he knew there was no use arguing.

Skippy was already keenly sensitive to all the family's moods. As Christmas drew near he was aware of a growing excitement in the house—a good, exhilarating kind of excitement. He could feel it in the way Mother smiled and hummed to herself as she went about her work; in Dad's boisterous greetings when he came home at night; in the whisperings that came from the boys' room after they had gone to bed. More than once he caught the parents tiptoeing up to the big attic closet with bulky, mysterious parcels.

There came an evening when the thrilling tension reached its peak. After supper Dad and the boys went out to the garage and came back carrying a woodsy-scented green balsam. This, the little dog decided, must be the great event everybody had been waiting for. He pranced around them while they set the tree up in the living room, and let off steam in a series of short, ecstatic barks.

But more wonders were to come. The children rushed for the stepladder and brought big cardboard boxes filled with colored balls and tinsel streamers. Long strands of wire, dotted with bright little lights, were festooned through the branches. Balancing on the upper step of the ladder and

Skippy's Family

reaching almost to the ceiling, Dad placed a cotton-wool angel high up in the tree, and a silvery tinsel star on the very topmost spire.

The children stood in hushed admiration.

"All right, now, my dears," said Mother, "it's time for bed. But hang your stockings up first, on this string in front of the fireplace."

When they finished pinning them in place there were five stockings in the row. At the end, beside Peggy Lu's sock, hung a shapeless bit of white cheesecloth, stitched together with red thread.

"What on earth is that?" queried Dad.

"It's Skippy's stocking," said John. "I cut it out an' Jane sewed it for me."

Hearing his name, Skip wagged his tail vigorously and tried to plant a wet caress on John's cheek. The little boy put an arm around his neck and led him quietly out to the

Skippy's Family

kitchen.

"Skip," he whispered, "if you keep listenin' hard all night, maybe you'll hear Santa Claus when he comes. I 'spec' he

wouldn't care if a little dog saw him. I tried but I guess I went to sleep. You can keep awake, can't you, huh?"

Whether or not Skip understood every word, he knew he was being urged to extra watchfulness. He answered with an eager little whine and darted off on a tour of the house, sniffing and listening at the doors, and even nosing under the

Skippy's Family

piano where he suspected a mouse had its lair.

Soon the children trooped off to bed and the dog was let out for his evening run. After making an unusually thorough inspection of the premises and finding nothing amiss, he returned to the front door and gave his customary bark, announcing that he was ready to come in. It seemed to take a long time for Dad to answer the summons. When he did appear he was tiptoeing in soft bedroom slippers and there were four or five sections of shiny toy railroad track in his hand.

Skip lay down on the rug and watched the strange proceedings. Dad was on his knees by the tree, puffing as he pieced together a long oval of track. Beside him were a bright little engine and cars, and a tiny red station with a green roof. Mother, meanwhile, was laying out piles of beribboned packages and murmuring quietly to herself ". . . that one must be from Aunt Marge . . . I *do* wish they'd tie the tags on tighter . . . Wonder what's in that queer-looking package for Jane?"

From time to time Skippy dozed. But he was wide awake when Dad and Mother turned the lights out and went cautiously upstairs.

Faithful to his trust, the little dog slept only in snatches and made the rounds every half hour the rest of the night. The whole quiet house was filled with the smell of the fir tree. Once, a little after midnight, there was a sound of singing voices far down Main Street. Skippy didn't bark. The

Skippy's Family

notes came clear and peaceful through the darkness, and he knew they boded no harm.

The crunch of wheels in the snow and the clink of the milkman's bottles before dawn gave him his first excuse to warn the household. Usually nobody paid any attention to those early-morning alarms, but now, to his amazement, there was a patter of feet on the stairs! Dashing in from the kitchen he found the three pajama-clad children rubbing their eyes in the lighted living room. There was a chorus of gasps and exclamations.

"Look! My 'lectric train! . . . An' a sled! . . . An' a Buddy-L steam shovel!"

Small John turned from the spectacle to Skippy, his blue eyes wide with awe. "Gee!" he whispered. "He did come, didn't he? An' you saw him! Gee!"

There were sounds of stirring overhead, and Dad's sleepy voice bellowing "Merry Christmas, kids!" And then the whole house seemed to explode in a bedlam of joyful shouts.

Dad and Mother came down, carrying Peggy Lu, and everybody talked and laughed at once.

"Can we have our stockings before breakfast, Mother?" Jane begged. "Just our stockings—we won't touch the big things."

At Mother's nod there was a scramble for the fireplace and each child began pulling small gifts out of his or her stocking. Not till he reached the orange in the toe did John

Skippy's Family

remember the fifth sock hanging above the hearth. He stared, then pointed. "I b'lieve Santa left sump'n for Skippy, too!" he cried.

And sure enough, in the little homemade stocking there were two dog biscuits and a rubber mouse!

That was Skippy's introduction to Christmas, and it was a day he never forgot. Through all his long life, the smell of Christmas trees and the rustle of Christmas wrappings made him gay and eager as any puppy. If he had any guilty feelings over the fact that he had napped through Santa's visit, he never showed them. After all, John believed the little dog had witnessed the good saint's arrival, and that was what counted.

* * *

As the weeks went by, Dad found that the children were still worried over Skippy's ownership. It was hard for them to believe that anyone—even the most heartless of men—could lose such a superior dog without taking vigorous steps to recover him.

Finally, to set their minds at rest, he had another talk with the Chief of Police. "It's

Skippy's Family

all right, kids," he reported when he came home. "The Chief says there hasn't been a single person asking about a dog like Skip. He thinks the poor pooch fell or was thrown out of some car that was traveling through. Anyhow, he belongs to us now. And just so everybody'll know it, see what I got for him!"

He held up a real leather collar, resplendent with brass studs and a brass name plate. That evening, surrounded by a breathless and bright-eyed trio, Dad carefully scratched letters on the brass with his penknife. "SKIPPY," he inscribed in capitals, and beneath the name he traced "565 E. Main St."

It was an amateurish piece of engraving, but to the admiring children it looked wonderful. For once they all agreed that theirs was one of the smartest daddies in the world.

Skip was less impressed. To him one strap around the neck was as much of a nuisance as another. When the old collar was removed he shook himself gratefully and dashed away before they could seize him. A general pursuit followed and at last he was cajoled into sitting still while the shining new adornment was buckled about his neck.

To Dad's continuing amazement, Skippy proved to be one of the best mannered dogs in the neighborhood. He was old enough to have outgrown the puppy habit of chewing up slippers, toys and other articles that came within his reach, and aside from his own rubber mouse he left such things strictly alone. He never had to be housebroken, and

Skippy's Family

he never chased automobiles.

On the other hand he had a few bad habits that needed correcting. One was his truculent attitude toward strange dogs. Regardless of their size he would attack them without hesitation if they so much as set a paw on the front lawn. Usually the speed and fury of his rush knocked them off their feet and sent them scampering away with their tails between their legs. Sometimes he got an ear torn or a paw nipped in the fracas, and limped back to the porch expecting the reward due a wounded hero. Dad's sternness on such occasions made him repentant for the time being, but never really overcame his instinct for battle.

He had to be punished, too, for his incurable hostility toward garbage men. Their usefulness was something which his doggy mind could never grasp. To him they remained thieves—intruders who periodically robbed the household of food. From the first sound of their heavy boots at the back door to the fading rumble of their truck down the street, he vented his righteous wrath in barks and growls. If he happened to be outdoors when they arrived, he snarled ferociously at their heels throughout the fragrant transfer of scraps from the family garbage can to the baskets they carried on their shoulders. And no matter how many times he was whipped for it, his enmity was never quenched.

As a rule he was obedient to orders. He understood not merely the words but the tone in which they were uttered, and responded accordingly. At the same time he had a strong

Skippy's Family

will of his own and exercised all his wiles to get his way. If he had been out for his evening run and was comfortably settled beside Dad's chair, any faintly interesting sound outside would bring him to his feet, alert. He would push his nose up under Dad's arm and whine and look expectantly toward the door. If this produced no result he would trot restlessly around the room, bark to attract Dad's attention, and exhibit every symptom of a dog in urgent need of being let out.

Finally Dad would sigh, put his work aside and start to rise. At the first sign of weakening Skip would prance up and down joyfully and lead the way to the front door.

One other vice he had which caused a permanent feud with Mother. That was his habit of scratching fleas on the oriental rug in the living room. Like all long-haired dogs he did have an occasional flea, and what more logical place could there be to scratch than in the warm comfort of the family's favorite gathering place?

At Mother's sharp "Skippy, stop that! Get off the rug!" he would cast a reproachful eye in her direction and stalk slowly and mournfully from the room.

Although he was bathed only at casual intervals, he was a remarkably clean dog. In winter he rolled in the fresh snow and in spring and summer in the grass of the lawn. And between times he licked his paws and the silky fringes on his legs and stomach till they were glossy bright.

Visitors were prone to admire him. Often a lady guest ex-

Skippy's Family

pressed a wish for just such a dog. "So pretty and affectionate, and so well-behaved!" she would say. "What breed is he?"

Then Dad would grin and scratch Skip behind one of his floppy ears. "It's rather a rare breed," he would explain. "A cross of collie, beagle, chow, spaniel and Irish terrier, with just a dash of Pekinese. Sort of a melting pot, in fact. I think the best thing to call him is an American."

FOUR

ONE of the gifts John received for Christmas that year was a sturdy little tricycle—a "bike," as he insisted on calling it. Jane already had a larger one, and Steve was the proud possessor of a real two-wheeler.

When warmer weather came, and the streets and sidewalks were free of snow, the three youngsters pedaled their way to school each morning. Steve led the way, riding grandly with only one hand—or even "no hands" if he felt particularly daring. Jane followed on her high tricycle. And last came John, his small, round legs pumping madly to stay in the procession.

Skippy had an overwhelming desire to go with them, and Mother was careful to have him safely in the house when the little caravan set forth. One day he fooled her. He hid behind the shrubbery and no amount of calling and whistling brought him to the door. When the children were a block away he stole out and tore after them, a brown streak of wilfulness, his ears streaming back in the wind.

Steve and Jane made a halfhearted effort to send him

Skippy's Family

home, but their voices lacked the ring of authority. When he completely ignored their commands, they accepted the situation with considerable cheerfulness. He trotted happily beside John's bike all the way down Main Street.

It was nearly a mile to the Friends' School. The two older children parked their wheels and went into the brick Elementary Building, and John trundled down the path to the low, white structure that housed the kindergarten and first grade. It was a pleasant, sunny building, nestling under the tall maples. Skippy stayed very close to the little boy's heels. From the open doorway he heard the friendly piping of childish voices and dashed forward joyfully. Before John could stop him he was inside—the center of an admiring group of children.

Later in the morning Mother drove downtown to do her marketing, and on the way she stopped at the school with an idea that she might solve the mystery of Skippy's disappearance. The first grade teacher greeted her with a broad smile.

"Yes," she said, "John's little dog is attending school today. But really, he's better behaved than most of my pupils! Except at recess time he hasn't moved an inch from that spot."

She pointed, and Mother saw Skip lying very quiet beside John's low chair. His limpid eyes rolled uncomfortably, refusing to meet her stern glance.

One word was all that was necessary. "Skippy," she said

Skippy's Family

reproachfully, and the dog rose. His head and tail drooped in shame as he walked slowly to the door. By the time Mother had made her apologies and returned to the car he was no more than a small, brown speck, trotting homeward, far up the street.

Skip never went inside the schoolhouse again. But every day for the rest of the term he left home promptly at quarter after ten and was gone for an hour. When this had been going on for a week, Mother decided to ask John about it.

"He comes to see me," the little boy told her. "Every day at recess he's sitting outside, waiting to play. But he's awful good. He doesn't come in, an' he doesn't bark. All the kids wish they had a dog as nice as Skippy."

* * *

By the end of January Peggy Lu was a year old and making ambitious efforts to walk and talk. She toddled about the house, much to the admiration of the older children, who picked her up and comforted her after her frequent tumbles.

One of the first words she learned to say was "Tippy." Whenever the dog was in sight she addressed him by that name—in shrill command or sweetly cajoling, as her mood might be. He would wag his tail uneasily or look to the baby's elders in mute appeal. That was because the first time he heard her call him he had rushed toward her and frightened her into loud tears.

Skippy's Family

It was John who decided that this state of affairs wouldn't do. One evening he took his tiny sister firmly by the hand and marched her across the living room to the corner where Skip was lying.

"Look, Peggy," he explained, "he's nice. He wouldn't hurt anybody. See how he likes me to pat him?"

Fascinated, Peggy Lu squatted on her heels and held out one wee, diffident finger. Half bold, half terrified, she thrust it toward the little dog's nose. Twice she pulled it back. Then in a moment of supreme daring she touched it to the tip of the moist, black muzzle. Nothing happened. Finding

Skippy's Family

herself unscathed, the baby girl squealed with glee and toddled off to tell Mother all about her exploit.

From that time on she had no more fear of Skippy. He became her much abused but willing slave, submitting without complaint to her unskillful caresses and confusing orders.

Dad used to laugh at them together. "As near as I can figure," he would tell his baby daughter, "you and Skip are just about the same age. I wish, though, that you'd hurry up and get as much sense as he has!"

* * *

The days grew longer and the sun shone warmer. Dandelions dotted the vivid green of the lawn. Dad and the chil-

dren went gaily about the spring work.

First there were the leaves to rake out of the corners and flower beds, and the screens to wash and put up. Then Dad got out the lawn-mower, oiled it and trimmed the swift-springing grass. Jane and John scratched the ground and planted small packets of seeds. And Skippy busied himself reburying bones and other hoarded treasures which he had been unable to hide properly in the frozen ground.

It was a good time of year. The whole horizon to the north was tinted with the pink of peach orchards in bloom, and in the field back of the house a sprinkle of white blossoms gave promise of wild strawberries. The children knew that as soon as the strawberries ripened, the end of school would be near. And then—the very first week of vacation—the family would be off to Pocono!

That was a subject they never tired of discussing. The lake, and the canoes, and the little "pumpkin-seed" sailboat; the hikes to the beaver pond and the Lower Tunkhannock; the deer that came down to drink by the lake shore at dusk; the chill mountain nights with a big log fire blazing on the hearth, and the snug double-decker bunks for dreamless sleeping.

As the day for departure approached, Dad made it clear that Skippy was not to accompany them. He had plenty of good reasons.

"Skip's a fine little dog for a place like this," he explained. "But up there in the deep woods he wouldn't know how to

Skippy's Family

behave. He might get lost or run over. And he'd surely get in trouble with those big dogs at the other camps."

John nodded unhappily. "I wish he could go," he said, "but I don't know whether he can swim. He might get drowned."

"Aw, sure he can swim!" Steve put in scornfully. "All dogs can swim."

"Well," said Dad in haste, "even if he can, there are too many other risks. He's happy here and you kids will have plenty of fun up there without him. You know how much he likes the Herrs, and they're fond of him, too. I've talked to Mr. Herr about it. He says they'll be delighted to keep him for the summer."

So it was settled.

School ended on a Thursday in the second week of June and by Friday night nearly all the preparations were completed. Dad carried out endless armfuls of quilts and blankets and sheets, stacking them compactly in the rear seat of the lumbering old Buick touring car. Suitcases and cardboard boxes full of clothes followed. The folding rack was attached to the left-hand running board and packed with still more luggage. Then the rear compartment of the little Whippet coupé was likewise loaded.

As soon as breakfast was eaten next morning, Mother and Ida Mae, the young nursemaid who was to go with them, began packing boxes of lunch and filling thermos jugs. And the youngsters raced about in a high state of excitement.

Skippy's Family

Skippy watched all this activity with an uneasy eye. When someone opened the screen door he slipped quietly out and disappeared. His absence went unnoticed until ten minutes later when Dad told the children it was time to take him over to the Herrs'.

All their searching, calling and whistling was to no avail. At last Steve happened to open the door of the Buick and there was Skip, crouched in the front seat. It took the combined efforts of all three youngsters to drag him out.

Dad stared at the unhappy little dog. "That's queer," he mused. "In all the months we've had him he's never been near one of the cars before. You'd almost think he knew we were going away."

"Of course he knows," said John. "I told him last night."

"Well, take him over to Mrs. Herr now," Dad replied. "And just to make sure he stays, you'd better shut him in their tool shed."

Sad-faced but obedient, the children carried their pet across the intervening lot and placed him on the dirt floor of the shed, latching the rickety door and hurrying away so that they wouldn't hear his pitiful whinings.

Five minutes later, when Dad came out with some additional items for the coupé, his eye chanced to fall on a small, furry object, huddled on the floor boards in a dark corner of the car. It was Skippy, his nose, breast and paws plastered with brown earth. He had dug his way out of his prison.

Dad was exasperated. They were almost ready to leave,

Skippy's Family

and something had to be done at once. He took a length of old clothesline, tied it firmly to the dog's collar and dragged him back to the Herrs'. There he made the cord fast to an apple tree and turned his back resolutely on those pleading eyes.

All the last minute tasks were done. The windows were shut and the house locked up. A cosy place was made for Ida Mae and the baby in the tonneau of the Buick beside the high-piled cargo. Steve and Jane scrambled in with Mother in front. Dad and John got into the Whippet.

"All set?" called Dad. "Okay—we're off!" And he started the engine, backing out of the driveway. The Buick was in motion, too, when John stood up suddenly and pointed.

"Look, Daddy!" he cried. "It's Skippy! He's on the running board!"

Dad honked the horn frantically and Mother stopped with a squeal of brakes.

"What's the matter?" she asked, flustered.

For a moment Dad didn't answer. He came and stood by the touring car and stared at the right-hand running board. Skippy cowered there, trembling but determined. A frayed, gnawed end of clothesline was still dangling from his collar.

"You little son-of-a-gun—" Dad choked. "By thunder, if you want to go that bad, we'll take you!"

FIVE

THE little dog quivered with fear and hope as Dad picked him up in his arms.

"Can he go, Daddy? Are we really going to take him?" chorused the children.

"If we didn't," said Dad gruffly, "the little cuss would probably try to follow us. Here, John, you hold him in your lap. Let's go!"

It was a hundred and ten miles from home to the lake. Dad chugged off in the lead in the little coupé, and Mother followed with the Buick. They drove through the level Jersey countryside, between green fields and trim orchards. At Palmyra they crossed the Delaware and threaded the traffic of U.S. Route 1, then angled up over the hills into Bucks County.

Skippy's trembling had stopped when he was safely in John's comforting arms. He sat there with his nose to the window, watching the road flow past. But when they had gone about twenty miles he began to twitch uneasily.

Dad glanced down. "What's the matter with him?" he

Skippy's Family

asked.

"I don't know," said John, "but I think he doesn't feel very well."

"Oh, gosh," said Dad. "Here, I'll pull over and stop and we'll let him out a minute."

But it was too late. Skip was violently ill all over John's playsuit, the seat and the floor. Dad parked beside the road and made such repairs as he could with an old newspaper while John tenderly nursed the invalid. Skippy was horribly embarrassed. The moment he began to feel better he looked up at them with such shame in his pleading eyes that Dad could find no words to rebuke him.

The Buick rolled up in the midst of the excitement and Steve and Jane ran over to offer the dog their sympathy. Mother, being more practical, produced a cloth moistened with water from one of the thermos jugs. In ten minutes the little caravan was on its way once more.

To say that poor Skippy enjoyed the

Skippy's Family

trip would be stretching the facts. He endured it stoically in spite of a still queasy stomach. Not for him the thrill of the unfolding hills above the Wind Gap, or the first sight of Big Pocono shouldering the sky. He drowsed unhappily in John's lap, and only once during the long journey did he show any interest. That was when Dad stopped the car at a gas station above Stillwater, where there were three half-grown bear cubs in a wooden cage. The little dog looked at them, sniffed their strange aroma and gave one feeble growl, then subsided into John's arms.

The two cars stopped for lunch beside a mountain brook a little off the highway. Then they climbed the last few miles to the Summit and rolled westward across the plateau. The woods grew thicker and the houses fewer. At last they turned in on a dirt road, dappled with pine shadows, that curved along the shore of the lake.

"Look, Skippy," breathed John. "It's Pocono! We're 'most there!"

The little camp was ready and waiting for them. Aunt Marge had come over from her near-by cottage to open all the windows and put a bowl of fresh flowers on the table. They parked the cars by the roadside and began carrying armfuls of supplies up the footpath to the door.

For a few moments Skip stood wanly by, recovering his land legs. Then his nose lifted to the lure of a dozen strange, intriguing scents. The breeze brought him news of ferns and hemlock thickets and small, bright-eyed creatures hiding

Skippy's Family

behind tree trunks. In a twinkling his late indisposition was forgotten. His tail flicked up, his ears cocked, and he darted off into the underbrush.

None of the children saw him go, for they had hurried to the house to get into their bathing suits. Soon they were racing down to the swimming dock, where half a dozen youngsters, including their cousins, were already cavorting. It was not until after countless dives, two swims to the buoy and back and a game of water tag that Steve remembered they had something to brag about.

"We gotta dog," he announced. "He's the slickest dog there ever was."

"His name's Skippy," added John.

"Where is he?" challenged a cousin skeptically.

"He's right here. We brought him up in the car," said Jane. "Here, Skip! Here, Skip!"

There was no answering bark, though they waited and watched, called and whistled.

"Well," said the cousin, "where is he? I should think he'd come if he's such a slick dog."

The three children were troubled, their truthfulness in question. Abandoning the dock and the joys of the water, they hastened up the path, still calling and searching.

But he wasn't in the house, and neither Mother nor Dad, busy with the unpacking and settling, had seen him for the past hour. The youngsters got into their clothes and set off in various directions to continue the hunt. Steve went west

Skippy's Family

and Jane east along the road. John made a sorrowful patrol of the reeds and bushes that fringed the shore, still bothered by a secret fear that the little dog had come to grief in the lake.

The sunny afternoon dragged on toward evening and no trace of Skippy could be found. At the children's insistence Dad got into the Whippet and drove for miles, stopping at various camps to question the neighbors. When he came back at suppertime his search had been unrewarded, and he was beginning to share the worries of his offspring.

It was a doleful meal they ate on the screened porch of the cabin. Even Dad's promise that they could go out on the lake with him to watch the sunset failed to banish the gloom. After supper a subdued little group helped launch the canoe. Steve took the bow seat and Dad the stern, while Jane and John squatted amidships.

They paddled out across the cove, where long shadows were beginning to darken the mirror-like surface. The whole western sky, above the woods, was rose and gold. The evening was so still that they could hear the notes of a hermit thrush deep in the forest and the splash of a fish jumping, farther up the cove.

Dad's peace was interrupted by a plaintive remark from

Skippy's Family

John, in the middle of the canoe. "It's awful pretty, Daddy, but we'd like to go back now."

"Yes," said Jane, "it's getting kind of cold, and besides—maybe we can find Skippy before it's too dark."

"All right," Dad agreed. "It does feel a bit chilly. I guess you kids ought to have sweaters on, so we'll go in."

He swung the canoe shoreward and drove the paddle deep. They had taken only a dozen strokes when Steve stopped paddling.

"Look." He pointed. "There's sump'n on the dock. I think—I think maybe it's Skip!"

John knew better than to stand up in a canoe but he began to squirm violently. "Gee!" he said. "I wish I could see, too. Holler at him, why don't you?"

Skippy's Family

"Skip—yea, Skip!" yelled Steve. "He's jumpin' up an' down. Hurry, Dad!"

When Dad put his back into it he could really make a canoe travel, and in a few moments they were swirling up to the side of the dock. When the little craft was still two or three yards away Skippy gave a flying leap and landed in the water, his forepaws clawing frantically at the gunwale.

Dad fished the dripping animal out and he proceeded to shake himself so thoroughly that all of them were drenched. When the canoe had been hauled up and they arrived at the camp, Mother laughed at the bedraggled crew.

"He came home a little while after you started," she said. "He was limping and very tired, but he wouldn't eat anything because you youngsters weren't here. He just put his nose to the ground and followed your tracks down to the lake."

John brought the pan of food from the kitchen and the little dog went at it as if he had been starved for a week. That evening he lay on the rough stone hearth in front of the open fire and slept the sleep of utter fatigue. Sometimes in his dreams he moaned a little, and his legs twitched as if he were running.

"I 'spec' he's dreaming about chasing a deer," murmured John, and Dad nodded.

"Shouldn't wonder," he said. "He's tired enough to have run all the way to Big Pocono and back. Maybe he did start a deer, back in the woods beyond the fire-line. If that's what happened I bet he learned something new about fast traveling."

Wherever Skippy had been that long afternoon, he was up bright and early next morning, none the worse for his

experience. Pocono, he tried to tell the family, was a grand place. After being proudly exhibited to the doubting cousins he was taken over to the clubhouse and introduced to various friends and neighbors who were chatting on the porch.

Mr. Cary, the superintendent, had an elderly Welsh terrier named Doodles. A naturally aggressive dog, he had been spoiled by the attentions of generations of summer people and now regarded the clubhouse premises as his private park.

The instant Doodles sighted Skippy outside on the lawn his gray hackles rose and he rushed forth, voicing his indig-

Skippy's Family

nation. Skip was on strange territory and unsure of his rights. He looked up at the children questioningly, then stood like a small bronze statue as the other dog approached. There was an electric moment while Doodles circled him, stiff-legged and on tiptoe, a string of insults rumbling in his throat. Then, with frightening suddenness, the two dogs merged in a snarling, snapping whirl of gray and brown.

Jane burst into tears. Steve and John made brave but futile efforts to grab their dog and pull him out of the brawl. But Skip's dander was up now. He fought like a little tiger and only Doodles' long experience as a fighter had kept him from being badly mauled by the time Mr. Cary hurried to the scene. With a firm hand the superintendent jerked the dogs apart and shut Doodles up in the office. When he came back he was chuckling.

"Well, kids," he said, "I heard you'd lost a dog. This ferocious animal couldn't be the one, could it?"

He knelt and helped the boys pat Skip's ruff back into place. The little dog's eyes had stopped blazing and he wagged his tail in friendship.

Mr. Cary nodded approval. "Skippy, you're all right," said he. "I don't believe you'll have much trouble with Doodles after this."

It turned out as he said, for though the old terrier never felt kindly toward Skip, he was careful to avoid open battle in their later meetings.

The children said good-by and marched gaily home to

Skippy's Family

boast of their champion's prowess.

Dad was troubled. "Are you sure he didn't start the fight?" he asked.

"No, honest he didn't, Daddy," they chorused. "He didn't do a thing. He just stood there until Doodles jumped at him."

"He was a perfec' little gentleman," John added solemnly.

From that day Skippy fitted so easily into the pattern of the family's life at Pocono that Dad sometimes wondered why he had ever considered leaving him at home. The dog went wherever the children went and joined in their games with unquenchable enthusiasm. Much of their time was spent in and on the water. Skip soon demonstrated that he could swim as well as any of them, and if they left the dock in the canoe or the little sailboat without him he would plunge in and paddle valiantly in their wake till he was taken aboard.

Dad left in the chill dawn on Monday morning and didn't return until late Friday night of each week. But he was at the lake Saturdays and Sundays and those were the days reserved for hikes and picnics.

Sometimes they took the Ravine Trail down the shore of the swift-flowing Tobyhanna below the dam. The path twisted through rhododendron jungles heavy with bloom, climbed steeply to the cliff at Red Rock and plunged again into shadowy hemlock forest beyond. The children had several secret picnic spots along the brawling stream, and up

Skippy's Family

on the ridge above the trail there were blueberries and blackberries waiting to be gathered.

Back from the lake in many directions ran other woods paths with fascinating names. Among them were the "Wildcat Trail," the "Wolf Spring Run Trail" and the "Beaver Dam Trail," each with its special attractions. And though Skippy never learned to read signboards or look for blazed trees he came to know all of them better than the oldest woodsman on the Preserve.

SIX

IN the succession of Pocono summers Skippy became a familiar figure to the whole community. Not only did some hundreds of cottagers recognize the sturdy, friendly little dog. He was equally well known to the creatures of the woods—the jays and nuthatches and grouse—the squirrels and foxes—the otter and the deer. With some he was on good terms, but with others—notably the squirrels and blue jays—he maintained an undying feud. Wherever he went in the forest their scoldings followed him.

His first encounter with a woodchuck was witnessed by Dad and Mother and became a lasting legend in the family chronicle.

Dad had been down at the lake and was coming up the path when he heard wild, excited barking from behind the camp. Then came Mother's voice calling Skippy in alarm. Dad ran around the side of the building and stopped short, shaking with silent laughter.

A dozen yards behind the house there was a tall pile of dead limbs and brush, used for kindling. In front of this

Skippy's Family

fortress the biggest woodchuck Dad had ever seen sat on its haunches, brandishing its short forelegs and hissing defiance through huge, chisel-like teeth.

Skippy faced the unknown intruder with daredevil courage tempered by native caution. Barking hoarsely he darted forward as if to tear his adversary limb from limb, then as swiftly drew back. The woodchuck repelled each charge with more threatening gestures and fiercer hisses, refusing to give an inch.

It was a demonstration in miniature

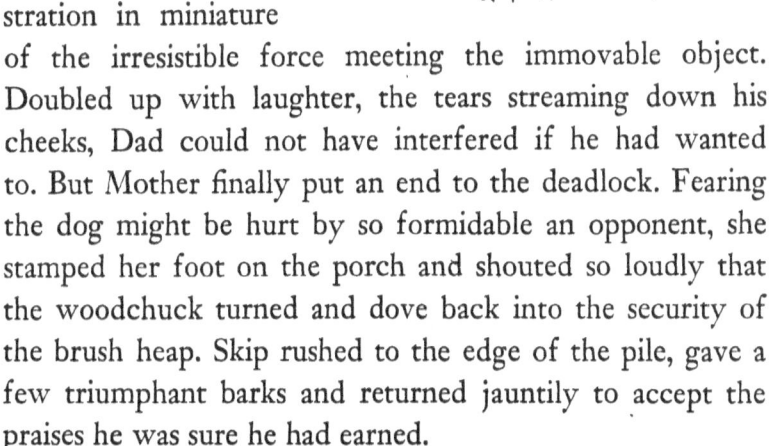

of the irresistible force meeting the immovable object. Doubled up with laughter, the tears streaming down his cheeks, Dad could not have interfered if he had wanted to. But Mother finally put an end to the deadlock. Fearing the dog might be hurt by so formidable an opponent, she stamped her foot on the porch and shouted so loudly that the woodchuck turned and dove back into the security of the brush heap. Skip rushed to the edge of the pile, gave a few triumphant barks and returned jauntily to accept the praises he was sure he had earned.

There were skunks in the neighborhood, too, as the family was occasionally informed by an unmistakable odor hang-

Skippy's Family

ing in the morning air. Mother worried for days after one of these visitations. She was sure Skippy would become involved in a battle that could end only in disaster. But by some miracle he avoided trouble. Possibly he had a tacit agreement with the black-and-white prowlers.

Donder and Blitzen, the twin Sealyhams next door, were less fortunate, perhaps because they had never been free to roam as Skippy had, and lacked his woods wisdom. Donder spent a whole week tied up in disgrace in a remote woodshed, and Blitzen was given five baths in two days.

In spite of the fact that Skip was allowed to wander as he liked over thousands of acres of wilderness, he never got lost or hurt while he was on the Preserve.

Only once, in half a dozen summers, did he fail to come home at nightfall. The children were bigger by then—Steve a lanky stripling, beginning to tinker with motorboat engines, and even Peggy Lu an accomplished swimmer and diver, aged four. But the consternation they all showed over the little dog's absence was as real as ever. John was out with a flashlight until long past his bedtime, trudging the road and whistling and calling.

Next morning it was a glum family that sat down to breakfast. They had planned an excursion to the Falls of the Tobyhanna, but nobody felt very enthusiastic about it.

"Well," said Mother, at length, "it won't do any good to stay here and worry about Skip. I'll pack the lunch and you boys had better paddle over to the main dock and get your

Skippy's Family

bathing trunks. Remember—you left them at the stockade after your swim yesterday. You'll need them down at the Falls."

The "stockade" was a log structure in the woods behind the clubhouse, used as a dressing room by the younger male population when they swam at the main dock. The two boys beached the canoe and went sadly up the path, their moccasined feet shuffling through the morning dew. Steve lifted the latch of the rickety door and pushed it open. He blinked in the semidarkness, then clutched John's arm.

"Lookit!" he gasped.

Something small and furry stirred on the bench below the hook where their bathing trunks hung. It jumped down, shook itself, yawned, stretched and trotted gaily across to welcome them.

The warmth of their hugs and the fervent pet names they called him seemed to surprise the little dog, but he returned their greeting with equal affection.

"I guess he followed us when we came up from the dock," said Steve sheepishly. "I sort o' remember he was around when we dressed."

"Crazy pooch!" John chided. "Why didn't you bark or sump'n when we shut the door—huh?"

But Skip was unconcerned. He had stayed with the bathing suits, sure that his young masters would come back. Now he raced ahead of them to the lake, lapped some water

Skippy's Family

thirstily, and jumped into the canoe, ready for a triumphal return.

* * *

That was the summer that John earned the nickname of "Beef." He had grown fast and in all directions. At nine he still had the tousled yellow curls, the cupid's bow mouth and the wide blue eyes of a particularly appealing cherub, but his body was as broad and chunky as a young Hereford steer's.

In July the family left Skippy behind and drove off to New Hampshire for a two weeks' visit at Grandpa's farm. The children had a glorious time, with the rambling house, the barn and a hundred acres of fields and woods to play in. There was a gangling 16-year-old farmer lad across the road who became Beef's idol. The stocky little boy followed his adored Baker with doglike devotion as he went about his chores.

One evening at the end of the first week Baker came panting up to the door with John on his shoulders. The child, he reported, had fallen from the haymow, when they were playing hide-and-seek, and hurt himself. Beef's round face was strangely white and drawn, and his arms hung at odd angles. He did not cry, either then or later, but Mother knew something was terribly wrong.

The doctor came, did what he could, and said X-rays would have to be taken immediately. At the little country hospital they made plates of both the boy's arms that night.

Skippy's Family

One—the right—showed a clean fracture of one forearm bone near the wrist. But the left elbow was so crushed and shattered that no local surgeon could set it.

The X-ray plates were rushed to Philadelphia and for four days John suffered and the family waited. Finally came word that a hospital room was ready and a well-known bone specialist would operate.

The big touring car was packed that night, and early in the morning they started. Beef sat beside his mother, his bandaged, splinted arms resting on half a dozen pillows. They raced the four hundred miles to Pocono and reached the lake before dark.

Skip must have recognized the sound of the car a quarter of a mile away. He was down by the roadside barking an uproarious welcome when they pulled to a stop. Then, at the sight of tired, anxious faces, he was silent. He stayed close by Beef's side, whining softly, as they moved up the path. And for the first time since his accident, the boy laughed.

"Good ol' Skippy!" he said. "Wish I could pat you, but you understand all about it."

Mother took John to the city next morning. He was in the hospital for three weeks and a housekeeper was sent up to the lake to look after the family. Those were trying days for everybody and Skip realized it. He went about with a subdued, troubled look in his expressive eyes, and got into as little mischief as possible.

Skippy's Family

It was a glad time when Beef came back, toward the end of the summer. He could stay only a day or two at a time, for he was still having regular treatments. But though his arms were still in a double sling, he was his happy self again.

Because he couldn't swim or play active games with the other youngsters, Skip became his constant companion. The bond between them, always close, grew stronger and deeper.

"Sometimes," said Mother, "it seems as if those two could talk to each other."

Beef had lost some of his sturdiness during those weeks in the hospital, and mild exercise was needed to build back his strength. Dad and Skip took him on hikes in the woods, that September. They would drive as far as the car could go, then start out on one of the forest trails, looking for such small adventures as might come their way.

One sunny afternoon they went to the beaver pond, hidden away in a swampy tract beyond the old sawmill. There was plenty of evidence of the beavers' work among the poplar saplings—neatly cut stumps and bits of wood that showed the clean chisel-markings of teeth. Skippy sniffed about, excited but wary. He didn't know just how big these creatures might turn out to be. After half an hour of patient watching they were rewarded by the sight of a blunt, brown head cleaving the water on the other side of the pond.

"Look!" cried Beef, and instantly the beaver slapped the surface with its tail and dove out of sight.

"I'm afraid that's the last we'll see of them," said Dad.

Skippy's Family

"That fellow gave the alarm, so they'll all lie low for a while. But I heard one of the kids say there's supposed to be another colony of beaver farther up the creek. I doubt

if we could find it, but a little exploring might be fun. How do you feel?"

"Swell," said Beef stoutly. "Let's go."

It was impossible to follow the creek, for it meandered through swampy thickets of alder and poplar that could not be traversed without hip boots and an ax. They took an abandoned wood road leading back from the sawmill and went up a hill where the sun hung in the pale gold of beech

Skippy's Family

leaves. Grass and bushes had grown up in the ancient ruts of the road and it was slow going for a boy with two broken arms.

They toiled up over the crest of a knoll and heard a sudden commotion ahead—a whirr of wings, a rustle of grass and a tiny, continuous peeping. Dad made a grab for Skip's collar and put a finger to his lips in a gesture of silence.

They caught a fleeting glimpse of half a dozen wee balls of yellow-brown fluff disappearing into the leaves. Then a

mother partridge tumbled toward them along the ground, squawking plaintively and trailing an apparently broken wing.

"Watch her!" whispered Dad. "She wants us to chase her —give the chicks a chance to hide."

Skip tugged frantically to get away and broke Dad's grip just as the brown bird fluttered to within a few yards. His rush missed her by a bare inch. With feigned clumsiness she rolled sidewise, fanned her wings in the dog's face and darted into the thicket where he could not follow.

Dad hurried forward to recapture Skip before he could nose out the babies hidden by the roadside. But at the very moment he seized the dog's collar another grouse hurtled

Skippy's Family

down into the road with a roar of wings. This was the cock —the father of the brood. He made his landing twenty feet away and strutted toward them belligerently. His tail feathers were spread wide and his ruff fluffed out so that he looked at least twice his actual size. He came forward with short, quick steps, his wings thrust out from his sides, like a boxer looking for an opening. And from his beak came a steady scolding sound.

Skippy was cowed by this show of fighting power. He whimpered and looked up at Dad as much as to say "Let's get out of here!"

Then the cock partridge made a threatening move toward Beef, who stood helpless, doubled up with laughter. That was different. Skip lunged forward, raging like a lion. No puffed-up bird was going to hurt his defenseless comrade. It was all Dad could do to hold him, for by this time he too was laughing so hard his sides ached.

"Come on, Beef," he gasped. "We'd better clear out before these bloodthirsty brutes slaughter each other."

Still chuckling, they turned and went back down the wood road. And Skippy trotted beside them, relief in every line of his shaggy little body.

SEVEN

WHEN the family returned from Pocono that fall, it was not to the brick house on East Main but to the "new house" on a pleasant side street at the other end of town. The "new house" was larger, more imposing than any they had ever lived in. And it was theirs—or at least they were buying it. The children were still awed by its white-stucco, pink-roofed magnificence, and Dad by the size of the mortgages and the area of lawn to be cut.

They had moved in January, one gray Saturday when there was snow on the ground and a threat of more in the air. The heavy furniture was carried by a local hauler's van, and Dad shuttled the two mile length of Main Street in the car a dozen times, transporting smaller articles that ranged from Peggy Lu's dolls to Petey, the canary.

Skippy rode with him on one or two of these trips. Disturbed by the upheaval at first, he had soon entered into the children's mood of bustle and excitement. He made a hasty inspection of the new house, sniffing at the bare walls, rugless, slippery floors and general air of bleakness, then devoted an hour to a more thorough exploration of the grounds

and shrubbery. Nobody asked him how he liked the place, for the entire family was busy. Dad, Mother, Ida Mae, and the little girls were occupied with the hectic details of getting settled, and Steve and John were out making new

Skippy's Family

friends in the neighborhood.

Evening came before they were ready for it. The beds were set up and some of the rugs down but the furniture was still placed helter-skelter and there were no pictures on the walls. Wearily they ate a scratched-together supper. By nine o'clock everybody was in bed but Dad. He stretched his aching back, fixed the fire for the night and went to lock the back door. It was then that he remembered Skippy. The little dog's bowl of food was still sitting untouched under the kitchen range.

"Here, Skip!" Dad called from the doorway. "Here, boy!"

He pursed his lips and sent a piercing whistle out into the night, but there was no answering bark. A light, dry snow was beginning to fall.

Dad fumed at the inconsiderateness of dogs, laid Skip's quilt in a sheltered corner of the back porch, turned out the lights and went to bed. He half expected to hear a plaintive request for admittance before he got to sleep, but he was too tired to wait for it. The next thing he knew it was broad daylight, with the sun shining on new snow.

At breakfast time Mother remembered she had left her garbage can at the brick house. "I'm sorry," she told Dad, "but I guess you'll have to make one more trip up there."

"All right," he said, resignedly. "By the way, has Skip been around this morning?"

"Why, no. I haven't seen him. Wasn't he in the house

Skippy's Family

last night?"

"No," said Dad. "But I have a sort of hunch I know where he was."

He got the car out of the garage and drove up Main Street through the snow. When he turned into the familiar driveway he began to chuckle. Down from the porch of the locked, empty house came Skippy, tail wagging with joy. There was a round, snowless patch close to the front door where he had spent the night, curled up in a furry ball.

The little dog jumped up on Dad and whined eagerly. "It's about time," he was trying to tell him. "About time you folks got some sense and came back to a comfortable place to live."

Dad nodded. "Look," he said, unlocking the front door. He waited a minute or two while Skip raced through the echoing interior. When the dog came back his eyes were sad and his tail drooped in disillusionment. Slowly he walked out to the car and climbed in. He never went back to the brick house again.

Skippy cheered up the moment he came into the new kitchen and smelled cooking and the people he knew. Even before he would taste his leftover supper he made a hasty investigation of the house and came back with a satisfied air. Everything was right with his world again.

The place on Colonial Avenue was really a superior location for dogs. The house had a broad, terraced lawn in front and the lot ran back to a lane in the rear. There were trees

Skippy's Family

and shrubbery and a fascinating vacant lot beyond the hedge, full of high weeds and grass that probably sheltered whole colonies of rabbits. Across the wide street, with its rows of scarlet oaks, a gnarled old apple orchard offered plenty of room for the burying of bones. And south and east of the property stretched miles of cornfields and woods. Best of all, there were very few cars or trucks and no buses to make life hazardous.

Skippy spent the next few days in happy exploration. There were just enough other dogs in the neighborhood to add spice to existence. Old Ches, the huge police dog, who lived down at the corner, for instance. Ches had owned the street for some years, and he was inclined to look down his nose at the little newcomer. But Skip stood for no nonsense when the old dog started to take his dignified way across the lawn. In one whirlwind round Skippy established his right of domain, and from that day on they treated each other with mutual respect.

In spring birds came to nest in the sycamores and maples, and the April air was melodious with song sparrow trills and  catbird calls. Skippy had no special interest in the feathered guests, but because of his inborn hatred of cats he did his

Skippy's Family

share in protecting the bird population. From sunset to bedtime he patrolled the premises, and night-prowling toms and tabbies learned to give the place a wide berth.

Only once in his long career did these police duties end in grief for the little dog. It was a warm May night, and Dad, reading late in the living room, heard the crooning yowl of a tomcat serenading his lady-love somewhere beyond the hedge. There was a patter of scampering feet and then a furious barking, as Skippy dashed to the attack.

After that something seemed to go wrong. This cat neither fled across lots nor took to a tree. Out of the night came a sound of snarling and spitting, and suddenly Skip's bark turned to a yelp of pained surprise. Dad dropped his book and hurried forth. On the moonlit terrace he met the little warrior returning in sorrow. His tail drooped and there was deep shame in the look he gave Dad with his one good eye. The other eye was closed and bleeding from a long claw slash.

Dad didn't give him the scolding he deserved. He carried him inside, washed the gash as well as he could, and anointed it with a mild antiseptic. It was two weeks before the wound

Skippy's Family

healed completely, and for the rest of his life Skippy was more cautious in his approach to cats.

The children shared his high opinion of the new neighborhood. They were growing like weeds, and to Dad's and Mother's consternation they seemed to change almost from day to day. Peggy Lu was a baby no longer, but a round-faced little girl with pigtails, starting off to kindergarten. Jane suddenly laid aside her dolls and devoted herself to field hockey and collecting little carved elephants.

The boys' changes of interest were even more frequent and more startling. Beef, kept out of strenuous athletics for a year while his left arm recovered its strength, went in for drawing long, low racing cars and building little models of airplanes and ships. His patient, clever fingers produced gifts for all his relatives that Christmas. Steve, meanwhile, had acquired a dilapidated Model-T Ford chassis from a junk dealer. The thing appeared in the back yard one day as the result of a mysterious transaction which Dad and Mother never quite understood. It involved the sum of three dollars in cash and other items taken in trade.

Dad resigned himself to the eyesore, figuring no harm could come from letting Steve tinker with its rusty parts. A month later he had a rude awakening when the 13-year-old was arrested for "operating a motor vehicle on the public highway without a license." The rejuvenated car was sold at a handsome profit, but from that moment Steve's consuming interest was in internal combustion engines.

Skippy's Family

The boys' restless imaginations led them into all sorts of experiments, and Skippy, trotting faithfully at their heels, was usually the uncomplaining victim. For years John tried to make the little dog a useful member of society by hitching him to sleds and coaster wagons. All sorts of harnesses were contrived for him, most often out of old clothesline. He would submit good-naturedly enough while they were strapped on him, but when it came to pulling he could be stubborn as any mule. With Beef running ahead of him he would follow joyfully. Then, the moment the boy took a seat on the wagon, Skip would lie down in the traces or scratch at an imaginary flea.

The day a pair of barnstorming aviators put on an exhibition at the little local airport was an ill-starred day for Skip. Steve and John returned from the show with ideas. One of the stunts they had witnessed was a parachute jump, and the following Saturday the two boys smuggled one of Mother's sheets out to the garage. They made cords fast to the four corners of the sheet, tied the loose ends to a brick, climbed to the garage roof on a ladder and tossed the bundle into the air. The parachute opened neatly and the brick landed on the lawn like a feather.

"Gee," said Beef, "it works swell! S'pose it would hold me?"

Steve looked critically at his chunky brother and decided in the negative. "We can try it with more bricks, though," he replied. "Just like test pilots. We'll find out the max'mum

Skippy's Family

load."

They dropped two bricks, then three, with moderate success. That was all the bricks they had, but Beef's roving eye fell on the hapless Skippy, who had been watching the proceedings with lighthearted interest.

The little dog looked troubled when he found both boys staring at him speculatively. He crouched and shivered when they tied the cords of the 'chute around his body. He whimpered and wriggled when they carried him up the ladder. Steve had one or two doubts when he reached the sloping roof, but Skippy felt light in his arms. After all, this was a scientific experiment in which sentiment had no place.

Unfortunately, the dog gave an extra squirm just as he was tossed into space, and his foreleg fouled one of the strings. Only half the sheet opened during the brief descent. Skippy landed on his side in the flower bed with a jolt that knocked the wind completely out of him.

Scared and contrite, the boys scrambled down the ladder and ran to their pet. He was still gasping for breath but he managed to get to his feet and stagger a few steps, dragging the parachute after him. Only when they had cuddled him and called him endearing names for ten minutes did the reproach in his eyes melt into forgiveness.

Skippy was stiff for a few days but he suffered no lasting damage. The next experiment in which he became unwillingly involved was more thrilling and less painful. Steve had

Skippy's Family

been helping Beef with his miniature airplane models. One day an ambitious idea flashed through his head.

"You know," he told his brother, "I bet we could build an airplane—a real one, big enough to carry us! Or anyhow, a glider."

With both the boys, action was never very far behind words. They toiled in a creative frenzy for two weeks, hiding their project from Dad's skeptical eyes by doing the work in a barn across the way. Finally they brought forth an actual glider. It was built of spruce sticks and muslin and piano wire—a biplane with a ten-foot wingspread. And to their fond eyes it was a thing of shining grace.

The contraption had no seat nor landing gear. In the center of the lower wing was a hole in which the aeronaut's body could be strapped, and the theory was that he would run until the lift of the wings bore him, kite-like, into the air.

Steve tied a thirty-foot towrope to the leading edge of the lower wing and fastened the other end to his bicycle. Beef was to have the glory of being the first to fly. With straps over his shoulders and about his chest, he strode out into the middle of the wide street, surrounded by thirty pounds of aircraft. Steve tested the direction of the wind and headed his bike into it.

"All set?" he called, and as the rope pulled taut he started pedaling furiously. It was hard pulling, and only after he got up speed did he look over his shoulder. There was Beef,

Skippy's Family

pounding along like mad, his mouth open and his face scarlet. But he was still on the ground.

They halted at the end of the street, and Beef sat down on the curb, glider and all. After a minute or two he found breath enough to speak. "I'm—too—heavy, I guess," he panted. "An' I can't—run—fast enough. I could—feel it lift, though."

Skippy, who had raced alongside, enjoying the spectacle, chose that moment to crawl up on the wing and lick John's perspiring face. It was a mistake, as he found out afterward. The boys exchanged understanding nods and took the glider back to the barn.

An hour later they had attached a pair of light baby-carriage wheels to the underside of the frame, and rigged a small seat amidships. With soft words they cajoled Skippy up onto the seat and tied him in place. Beef laughed at the droll expression on the little dog's face. "He looks just like he used to when we rode him in the doll coach," he said.

They trundled the glider out to the head of the street once more. The breeze had stiffened. Steve mounted his bicycle and Beef went around behind to steady the tail of the machine. After the first few wobbly yards the glider straightened itself and soon Steve was pulling it faster than Beef could run. He saw the wheels bounce once or twice, then rise slowly into the air. The boy let out a triumphant whoop as the flimsy craft soared along, a yard above the pavement.

At the sound, Steve turned his head. His front wheel hit

Skippy's Family

a stone and zigzagged to the right. And the glider swerved suddenly in the same direction, crashing one wing into rags and splinters against a tree. Skip was catapulted free and landed, scared but unharmed, on a neighbor's lawn.

Unfortunately there had been no other witnesses to the flight, and although the glider was patched up it never performed successfully again. The boys had a hard time convincing parents and schoolmates of their exploit, but they stuck manfully to their story. Skippy, they claimed, was the only flying dog in New Jersey.

EIGHT

NOBODY ever succeeded in teaching Skip to do tricks. Perhaps nobody in the family had the necessary patience. But the boys had another theory. After trying for half an hour to educate him in the art of shaking hands, Steve once offered the opinion that the little dog was just too intelligent to learn.

What gave weight to this judgment was the roguish perversity with which Skippy eyed his would-be instructors. He certainly understood their commands and pleadings, but if he couldn't see the sense in an order he simply ignored it. When a stick or a tennis ball was thrown for him to fetch, he would go after it and bring it back once—but only once. He knew well enough that the second toss was no accident. He would give the thrower a look of disdain and trot off to more interesting pursuits.

There were other games, however, that he never tired of playing. Football was one. When Dad and the boys started passing the pigskin on Saturday afternoons in the fall, Skip joined in the sport with enthusiasm. Let the ball once slip

Skippy's Family

from unwary fingers and the dog was on it like a pouncing catamount. He would roll with it down the terrace, pawing and mouthing the leather while he growled ferociously. His

fondness for chasing footballs probably helped to make the youngsters more adept at pass-catching.

Skippy's other favorite sport was rough-and-tumble wrestling. As the boys grew up they were closely matched in strength, though not in build. Steve was lean, broad-shouldered, long-armed and wiry. Beef, when his baby fat had turned to muscle, was solid brawn. He had an advantage in

Skippy's Family

weight that offset the three years' difference in their ages. Both loving physical combat, they engaged in almost daily wrestling and sparring bouts, and to Mother's disgust, these usually took place on the big rug in the living room.

There would come a time in the evening when homework became a bore. Dad, trying to finish a chapter in the corner, with his writing board and manuscript across his knees, would be startled by a floor-shaking thud and look up to see a thrashing, laughing tangle of boys on the rug. He would get up with a sigh, move lamps and coffee tables to places of safety, and go back to his stint. But by this time there was always a third party in the struggle. Skip would roar in from the kitchen, or wherever he happened to be, and join forces with either boy who might be getting the worst of it at the moment.

He could not bear to see one of his idols in trouble, even at the hands of the other. He would attack whichever lad was on top, worrying at an arm or a leg without actually doing any biting. Finally, when both boys were out of breath, they would roll over and start mauling the little dog, to his complete delight. He thoroughly enjoyed being tossed over and over or end for end, having his fur roughed up and his ears pulled. When it was over for the evening he would pantingly plead for more.

There was only one thing of which Skippy was really afraid. That was the noise of guns. Possibly he had been shot at when he was a puppy—back in that unknown past of his

Skippy's Family

which was always a subject of family speculation. At any rate a loud banging noise would send the little dog scurrying for cover. He very rarely visited the second floor, but on such occasions as the Fourth of July, or the opening of the rabbit season, he scrambled nervously upstairs and lay huddled under Dad's bed.

Thunderstorms had a similar effect on him. Even the most distant rumble of summer thunder turned him into a coward. When the boys were big enough to handle firearms, each was allowed to have a twenty-two rifle. They had expected Skip to be their trusty hunting companion, but when they set out after crows or bullfrogs they could never find him. One glimpse of the rifles being taken from the closet and he quietly disappeared.

"It's his ears," Beef explained, defending him. "He's got very sensitive ears. And it's not just guns, either. Look how he acts when Dad plays the mouth organ!"

There was no question about the disturbing quality of Dad's harmonica solos. However softly he played, the little dog would rush into the room before he could finish two bars. Showing every sign of agitation, Skip always started a singsong accompaniment of complaint that continued until the music stopped. When Dad was rendering some of the more melancholy airs, like "Old Black Joe," and "Massa's in de Cold, Cold Ground," Skippy's muzzle would point ceilingward and he would howl sadly, a little off key.

All this was hard on the vanity of the head of the house,

Skippy's Family

for the dog never paid the slightest attention to the radio, or to pieces the girls played on the piano. Dad had a secret yearning for musical expression, and the humble instrument he played was his only means of gratifying it. He finally reached a point where, if he felt a spell of mouth organ playing coming on, he would quietly usher Skip out of the house in advance.

Once there came a golden opportunity to vindicate his musical talents and silence the taunts of the family. Listening to the radio, Dad heard the announcement that the following number would be a harmonica selection by Mr. Larry Adler. Bounding from his chair he called Mother and the children as witnesses and planted Skip directly in front of the loudspeaker.

"Now," he said, "we'll find out about this. Mr. Adler is

Skippy's Family

a famous artist."

From the radio came a flood of pure tone—a Bach prelude handled with the virtuosity of a symphony orchestra. Skippy looked about with a bored air, scratched absent-mindedly behind his ear and flopped on the rug for a nap. Poor Dad! He never quite forgave the little dog for that blow to his pride.

During those middle years, a typical day in Skip's life began at 6:30, when Mother got up. He would be waiting by the door, ready to go out. In good or even moderately bad weather he stayed outside for fifteen or twenty minutes, giving the premises a pretty thorough going-over. If it was pouring rain he cut his tour to five minutes.

Reappearing at the front door at 6:45 he barked to be let in, went directly to the kitchen and had a good big drink of water. Then he stayed attentively close to Mother's heels until he was given his two dog biscuits and sent outdoors again. The biscuits were bone-shaped and tasted—as Beef reported after eating one—a little like stale ginger cookies without the ginger.

They were beautifully hard and had to be cracked with the back teeth. This Skippy proceeded to do to one of them,

Skippy's Family

bolting the pieces and licking up the crumbs. The second biscuit was a different matter. He eyed it and sniffed it thoughtfully, picked it up in his mouth and trotted across the back yard. In the midst of this journey he usually hesitated, starting in one direction, changing his mind, stopping and considering.

Once he had decided on the right place he looked all about, suspicious of observers, then hurried off into the shrubbery. The biscuit had to be concealed in a safe spot where he could return later for a light snack.

At 7:30 he was back, to be with the family at breakfast. Mealtimes were important occasions in his day, never missed if he could help it. He got no morsels from the table, but he loved the smells and sounds of eating. His favorite spot whenever a meal was in progress was in the doorway between kitchen and dining room—a vantage point from which his senses could take in everything, and where he was a continual menace to people carrying dishes.

He went out when Dad started for the bus at 8, and accompanied him part way down the street, returning leisurely to see the youngsters off to school. Only when they were safely on their way did the real business of his day begin. This was his regular round of calls on the town at large.

The way he invariably took was out the back lane, across half a dozen deep yards and vacant lots, and so at last to Main Street. No one ever followed him on these excursions, and so it would be impossible to map his exact progress. But

Skippy's Family

it must have involved visits to one or two hundred trees, lampposts and other points of interest.

If Mother drove uptown to do her marketing in the mid-

dle of the morning, she was almost sure to see the sober little dog jogging along the sidewalk a mile or so from home, or crossing the busy thoroughfare at his unperturbed trot, regardless of traffic.

The mailman had more exact knowledge of Skippy's movements. "I guess his route's about the same as mine," he

Skippy's Family

told Dad once. "Maybe a little longer, an' a few more stops, but he covers pretty much the same territory. I'll catch sight of him half a dozen times most mornings."

Skip was almost always back by 12 o'clock, and he spent the early afternoons snoozing comfortably in the sun porch or on his pillow in the old wicker armchair that was now reserved for his special bed.

Ten minutes before the youngsters came whooping home from school he was up and out again, waiting for them at the corner. From then until dinnertime he was as much in their company as possible, and of course he was on hand when the evening meal was served. The big moment of his day arrived when the family rose from the table and just before the dishes were washed. That was when he got his supper—a bowl of canned dog food with a few choice scraps of meat and vegetables added.

If no fresh bone accompanied the meal, Skip hurried out as soon as he had finished and dug up one of the dozen or more choice old ones he had conveniently hidden about the place. He usually made at least one attempt to bring the delicacy into the house. To his mind the proper place to enjoy a well-ripened bone was on one of the rugs. Of course it was strictly forbidden. But after years of firm denial, he still tried.

The family could always tell when he asked to be admitted with a bone in his mouth. It gave his bark a strange, muffled quality, like a muted cornet. But Skip was wily.

Skippy's Family

When nobody came to the door he would remain quiet a minute, then bark again in his normal voice, obviously innocent of any evil intent. Sometimes it worked. Mother would open the door a crack, see that the dog had no bone, and decide to let him in. All in one quick motion Skippy would snatch up the treasure he had concealed below the sill and dash inside, only to be driven forth with scoldings a moment later.

His evenings were spent in the society of the family. If by chance everybody went out to a movie or a school play, Skip was left to guard the house. Doubtless he did a good job of it, but he also used these rare occasions to enjoy a secret vice. Alone in the house, he went upstairs to the guest room and lolled in guilty luxury in the middle of Mother's best bedspread. No amount of scolding or punishment could cure him of the habit. And as the family was usually late getting started, nobody ever thought to close all the bedroom doors.

When the car drove in, his alert ear caught the sound of the tires on cinders and he was downstairs in a flash, waiting for the key to be turned in the lock. He always looked smugly virtuous, and welcomed the returning ones with a great deal of tail wagging. Only a hair or two and a slight depression on the surface of the guest-room bed bore witness to his wrongdoing.

Once, however, he was less fortunate. Coming home through a light snowfall, the car glided into the garage with-

Skippy's Family

out a sound. There was no conversation as the family came to the back door and opened it. Then Mother, who was in the lead, looked around the kitchen in surprise.

"Why," she said, "where's Skippy? Do you suppose—"

At that moment there was a hollow *thump* on the second floor, and a patter of hurrying feet on the stairs. In the front hall Mother looked down accusingly at the most crestfallen dog ever caught in crime. Skip refused to meet her glance. He made himself as small as possible and crawled past her into a dark corner under the kitchen table.

NINE

IT was amazing how rapidly the children grew up in those years, while Skippy seemed to remain completely unchanged. In no time at all Steve was a Senior and Jane a Junior in High School. To Beef's intense disgust, his elder brother had developed an interest in girls and got a tuxedo for Christmas. And Jane—now generally known as Pinkie—tripped grandly out to parties in a long evening dress. Peggy Lu was still a little girl, but her pigtails were gone and her brown hair bobbed.

It was a momentous day when Steve's seventeenth birthday came and he got his driver's license. Months before, he had bought a wrecked Model-A roadster. By dint of many expeditions to local junk yards he repaired the little car, tuned its engine and had it ready for the great event. In some way that Dad never inquired into too deeply, the boy was already an accomplished motorist. He learned the traffic laws by heart, passed his tests with flying colors, and came home proud and beaming, the possessor of an official driver's card. From that time on, he drove the children to school each day.

Skippy's Family

Those were the bottom years of the depression. It hit Dad's business a little later than some others, and while he kept his job he took a heavy cut in salary. Skip was more aware than the children that something was wrong. He knew

Mother worked harder, with no maid in the house. And he knew Dad sat up later in the evenings, trying to write the short stories that would help to pay bills. Sometimes when Dad stared sickly at the balance in his checkbook, Skippy would steal close to his chair and try to lick his hand.

They gave up Pocono that year. But when the hot weather came there was canoeing on the Rancocas and an occasional evening swim at a little lake in the Pines. Once

Skippy's Family

or twice the family drove to the beach for a week end, leaving Skippy with the local veterinarian, who maintained a small boarding kennel.

Those were low points in Skippy's existence. He detested the cramped quarters, the unfamiliar food and the casual ministrations of the kind but busy stranger who took care of him. Probably he was haunted, too, by a fear that this change in his life might be permanent.

When the sunburned family drove into the vet's yard at dusk of a hot Sunday night, there was a glorious reunion. Skip knew the sound of the car and barked frantically, clawing at the wire of his pen. Let out, he was like a crazy dog. He tore around and around the car, leaped high in the air to lick beloved faces, and shook himself violently to get rid of the hated prison smell.

In the fall there came another big event in the family's life. Enough cash had been scraped together to send Steve off to college. When the time came, Mother and Dad knew a solemn moment, for this was the first break in the ranks. Skip watched the new trunk being packed and heard the good-bys said. But it wasn't until Steve had been gone a day or two that he realized what had happened. He went up and sniffed at Steve's bed, at his old shoes and greasy coveralls in the closet. And from that time on he stayed closer than ever to Beef.

As it turned out, the separation from Steve was only temporary. When he came home in June he knew that he didn't

Skippy's Family

want to go back to college. His whole ambition was along mechanical lines and he wanted to get a job where he could use his hands. That wasn't easy, with some ten million Americans unemployed, but he did odd jobs around garages and filling stations that summer, tinkered with his car, and filled in as a truck driver.

When September came, it was Jane's turn to leave for college. Skippy missed her, too, but there were other things even more upsetting to the even course of his existence. Three or four nights a week, that winter, Steve would eat a hasty supper in the late afternoon, get into the cab of a big trailer-truck, and drive a hundred miles to the Pennsyl-. vania coal mines. About five in the morning he would come rolling in, practically dead on his feet from the long night's driving.

Skippy didn't do much sleeping those winter nights. He prowled the house, listening for the sound of the engine and the familiar step at the door. Sometimes, when there was fog or the roads were icy, he shared the strain with Mother, and hardly slept at all.

By spring Steve had a steady job as a service mechanic at the local Ford agency, and the grueling nights were over. The phase that followed was nearly as bad, however. Speed was in Steve's blood. He bought an old motorcycle and joined a club which went in for contest riding. Skippy spent several Saturdays under Dad's bed while the engine was being tuned up, for the roaring and banging were worse

Skippy's Family

than a dozen July Fourths.

The family, like the country, was beginning to get back on its feet that year, but there were disturbing signs on the European horizon. Skippy couldn't read the papers but he could read the frown of foreboding on Dad's face as he lis-

tened to the radio or studied news reports. As the summer passed, however, there were other matters to occupy the little dog's mind. He was eleven years old now—sedate and settled in his habits. His black face was touched with gray hairs, giving him a look of venerable wisdom. And he had been so long a member of the family that he took his rights and privileges for granted.

In August there was a rabies scare. A town ordinance ruled all dogs off the streets unless they were wearing muz-

Skippy's Family

zles. Dad went out dutifully and bought Skippy a heavy wire head-cage that looked like a catcher's mask. After a struggle it was buckled back of Skip's ears and he was turned loose in the back yard.

Three minutes later, impatient barking summoned Dad to the door. There was Skippy, a shapeless tangle of bent wire dangling from a strap about his neck.

Dad returned to the hardware store and got another muzzle—an old-fashioned leather one that lasted nearly two hours after it was put on. The little dog had clawed it with a hind foot until the strap slipped over his lower jaw, then chewed it through. That ended the muzzles, but Skippy spent the next two weeks on a leash that slipped along the clothesline and gave him a fair section of the yard to run in. He didn't like it. Most of the time he lay moping on the back steps.

Hardly had he enjoyed his first day of freedom after the ban was lifted when his well-ordered world was shaken again—this time by a real cataclysm. Steve rode home one evening on his motorcycle with a strange-looking bulge in the bosom of his leather jacket. Queer little squeaking noises came from it as he hurried into the house.

"Maw!" he called exuberantly. "Look what Skeets gave me!"

Carefully he opened his jacket and deposited on the kitchen floor a tiny, fat, furry bundle.

"Remember, I was telling you about Lady having pups?" Steve went on happily. "This is the cutest one. Isn't he cute, Maw—huh?"

Skippy's Family

Mother patted the wee dog with some misgivings. "He looks awfully young," she said.

"Four weeks," Steve replied. "But Lady's got so many she can't feed him. He's learning to lap milk out of a saucer. You don't need to worry, Maw. I'll take care of him an' feed him an' everything."

Mother smiled, a bit grimly. "You may as well start now," she told the boy. "Get some water and a mop and clean up that puddle."

Skippy sniffed at the small stranger with distaste, then yawned and went off to his chair for a nap. He didn't realize yet that the puppy had come to stay.

That night the family gathered in the basement to admire the newcomer. There was no denying his appealing qualities. Most of his coat was a dark brindle, almost black, but he had a white nose, a broad white collar and two white front feet. There was a snowy echo at the tip of his funny little tail.

"One thing I don't quite understand," said Mother. "Lady's such a beautiful buff and white collie. He's not colored at all like her."

"No," Steve admitted. "Must have been a slip somewhere. Skeets thinks the pup's pappy was probably a brindled Boston bull."

"What are you gonna name him?" asked Beef.

The whole family had been to see the movie, "Brother Rat," the night before.

"How about calling him Misto?" Mother suggested. "Re-

Skippy's Family

member the little fat cadet who was always falling over his own feet? This puppy makes me think of him—clumsy and affectionate and—"

"Right!" said Dad, who had been working on a show-dog story. "We can explain that Misto is short for his bench name—Champion Mistake of Battersby."

Amid a chorus of approval, Steve squatted and snapped his fingers. "Come on, Misto—come on here, boy!" And with a squeak that was meant to be a bark, the puppy waddled toward him joyously on short, weak legs. His christening was over.

On the cellar stairs there was a hasty patter of feet. Skip had waked up in time to hear laughter and talk in the basement. He hurried into the midst of the group and gave the little stranger a thorough inspection. Misto pushed against him without fear, nuzzling hopefully at the larger dog's furry underside.

There was excitement tinged with alarm in Skippy's eyes as he looked at Mother and Dad and the children in turn. A flash of understanding had told him this was a permanent change in the household—that his whole manner of life would have to be readjusted. He gave the family a glance of reproach and stalked off upstairs again.

For the moment nobody paid much attention to the old dog's injured feelings. The roly-poly Misto was still the center of interest. A box was prepared for him, he was fed some warm milk from a saucer, and finally they left him whimper-

Skippy's Family

ing lonesomely in the warm darkness.

All through that first night plaintive little squeakings came from the cellar, disturbing Skippy's slumbers. In the morning he went down again with Steve to make sure the puppy was flesh and blood and no dream. In a moment he returned, wrinkling his nose. No words could have expressed more clearly his disapproval of Misto's lack of training.

Skippy's routine was forgotten that day. Instead of trotting off for his usual tour of the town after breakfast, he asked to be let in. The puppy seemed to hold a strange fascination for him. He went to the sun porch, where Misto had been placed among plenty of newspapers, and lay down where he could observe all the baby dog's maneuvers.

Misto made laborious journeys under the chairs and the table, giving bright-eyed scrutiny to all his new world. Occasionally his mouth would open in a wee, pink yawn and then he would flop over on his side for a few winks of sleep. At intervals Skippy got up and nosed the puppy, curiously but without malice. Once, when Misto strayed off the newspapers and a *faux pas* seemed imminent, Mother saw Skip push the plump infant back to safer territory. She was still chuckling about it when Dad came home.

"Skippy," she said, "is trying to bring up Misto. He's like a fussy old bachelor suddenly presented with a baby to raise. If Skip's nerves hold out, that puppy ought to be a model dog."

TEN

MISTO thrived and grew amazingly. After the first few futile attempts to obtain nourishment from Skippy, he decided the larger dog was not his mother after all and devoted himself to lapping up a saucer of milk half a dozen times a day. His stomach was round as a drum and it seemed to the family that he increased in size day by day.

By the time he had been with them three weeks, and was reasonably well housebroken, he was almost half as big as Skippy. And from then on the old dog had to lead a more active life than he had known for years. Misto wanted to play all day long. He would crouch and bark ferociously, then pounce on Skip, nipping an ear or a paw with his tiny milk teeth. Up to a certain point, Skippy enjoyed the wrestling and mauling, but he got tired of it after an hour or two. Sometimes he would come to Mother with a harassed look in his eyes, begging to be rid of that black and white bundle of energy.

And still the puppy grew. His nose lengthened and he

Skippy's Family

began to look more like a collie. His legs stretched out and his paws became big and clumsy. By Thanksgiving he stood inches taller than Skippy, and weighed half again as much. Those were the days when the old dog was really run ragged. For Misto had lost none of his zest for games of tag and rough-and-tumble play. Skippy became gaunt and worn, and each night as soon as supper was over he fell exhausted on his pillow.

Misto, Mother insisted, was an outdoor dog. "I'd as soon have a cow in the house," she said, "as this great, awkward thing."

So a kennel was built for the young dog and installed on the back porch, where its entrance was sheltered from the snow. Misto slept in it contentedly, rising only once or twice each night for a sortie around the premises. He accepted his new quarters, just as he did baths and whippings, without complaint. The family was never quite sure whether he was too good-natured or too scatterbrained to care.

In the winter evenings the living room was a place of turmoil. Beef was a Freshman at college now, beginning to make a name for himself in football and wrestling. On week ends when he came home, the boys were never happy unless they had both dogs in to romp with them, and Misto, now as big as a full-grown collie and with a stride like a trotting horse, was continually knocking things over.

One night, after a particularly strenuous session, Beef took pity on the panting Skippy and sat down in the big chair by

Skippy's Family

the radio with the old dog snuggled in his arms. He was fondling Skip's ears and calling him some of the foolish pet names he and Steve had long ago invented, when Misto ambled up.

Slobbering with unrequited affection, the overgrown pup planted his paws on John's knees and tried to get in on the petting.

"Nothing doing!" the boy laughed. "Go on, you big ox—beat it!"

Misto turned his head, looked across to the opposite corner of the room, where Mother sat peacefully knitting, and crossed the intervening space in two great leaps. Taking off from the middle of the rug, he sailed the last few feet through the air. All seventy-five pounds of him landed in a sprawl on Mother's lap, hurling knitting needles far and wide.

Not only was Mother too startled to scream—all the breath had been knocked out of her, as well. By the time she had been rescued and her knitting retrieved, she was laughing too hard to be angry.

Without question, Misto was a born clown. He kept the family in stitches with his clumsy antics. Compared to Skippy's, his eyes were small and unexpressive, but there was always a good-humored grin on his long, white-blazed face. Among the other dogs of the neighborhood he was a tremendous social success. His size and energy, combined with an innocent, puppy playfulness, made him the admired

Skippy's Family

center of any canine gathering.

When the moonlit nights of early spring came, Misto took to wandering. Dad had never thought it necessary to tie the young dog up, but one March morning he was missing at breakfast time. Beef rode his bicycle all over town without sighting the stray. Not until the morning of the second day did he turn up. It had begun to rain and blow in the night— a typical March northeaster—and Misto was a sorry spectacle when he barked hoarsely at the back door. His coat was a sodden mass of mud and cockleburs, and his feet were black with sticky tar.

It took hours to clean the dog up. At first the tar was a mystery. Then Steve remembered there was a road under repair, five miles across country to the south. Apparently Misto's rambles had taken him a long way.

Skippy greeted the returning prodigal with obvious pleasure and relief. He had been restless during Misto's absence, and as soon as the tired young dog had been fed and bathed, Skip stayed at his side, solicitous as any maiden aunt.

As if to show that he was repentant, Misto outdid himself in good behavior for the next few weeks. The family even began to think he was learning some sense and turning into a first-class dog.

But in June the *wanderlust* caught him again. This time his disappearance lasted nearly three days. When he staggered into the yard, late one afternoon, it was obvious that something was wrong. Brought into the kitchen, he lay dull-eyed and refused both food and water. A feeble wag of the tail was his only response to Skippy's affectionate welcome.

Dad thought he might have been hit by a car, but a careful examination revealed no broken bones, no cuts or bruises. In the morning they took him to the vet. Various heroic remedies were tried without effect. Twenty-four hours later the young dog was dead. Something he had eaten—chicken bones, perhaps—had caused a stoppage of the intestine and ended his happy-go-lucky existence.

Skippy missed his big playmate. And because the family felt the loss too, the old dog came in for more than his usual share of petting and attention. With advancing age he had become something of a trial to Mother, who had to interrupt her work twenty times a day to let him in or out. But she understood his lonesomeness and put up with his whims. Nobody could stay cross at Skippy for very long. One look from his sad eyes was enough to wring sympathy from the hardest heart.

That summer the family went back to Pocono after an absence of several years. It was like a tonic to Skip. His mounting excitement could be seen in the eager lift of his ears and the quivering of his nostrils as the car entered the Preserve. Next morning he was like a puppy again, racing through the cool, green woods.

He was nowhere in sight when Dad and Beef took the canoe out for a trip to the head of the lake. They had paddled something over a mile against a crisp morning breeze,

when Beef chanced to look astern.

"There's an animal swimming back there by the point," he said.

Dad shipped his paddle and shaded his eyes, staring across the choppy, blue water. In the distance he made out a dark dot moving in their direction.

"Too small for a deer," he said. "Looks more like a beaver, only it's not making much headway. Could be a dog. Say—do you suppose—"

Beef was already swinging the bow around. They drove the canoe hard, their eyes on the small, dark head that disappeared now and then under a sloshing whitecap.

"It's Skip all right," said Beef. "If the crazy old pooch followed us all the way, he must be about done."

When they were within twenty yards they could see that Skippy was in bad shape. Still pawing feebly at the water, he was having a hard time keeping his nose above the waves. More than once he was battered under for seconds at a time.

It was a very tired dog that they hauled into the canoe. When Beef lifted him by the hind legs and thumped his chest, water poured out of his slack jaws. He choked once or twice and began to breathe wheezily, lying in the bottom of the canoe. Ten minutes passed before he had the strength even to shake himself.

"I don't know what made me look around," Beef growled, "but I guess it's a good thing for you I did—you brainless old dope, you!"

Skippy's Family

Skippy recovered from his near drowning without any ill effects. By the time they returned from the cove at the head of the lake he was standing with his forepaws on the center thwart, watching the shore with all his usual zest.

"I wonder," Dad mused, looking at the dog's determined back, "whether he's learned his lesson."

Beef chuckled. "Not Skip! He'd do it again in a minute."

For the rest of their stay at the lake they were careful to find Skippy and take him aboard before they went anywhere by water.

He came home from the vacation lean and hard and full of energy. Though he had lived with the family nearly thirteen years, he had never grown fat, probably because he was never overfed or given sweets. The first illness in his long career came that winter, when an infected molar swelled one of his cheeks. The vet who pulled the tooth was an old friend.

"Never saw a dog in better condition at his age," he remarked. "Anybody looking at that glossy coat and those teeth would think he was a six-year-old. I shouldn't wonder if he'd be with you for quite a while yet."

ELEVEN

THERE was a restless uncertainty in the air, that winter of 1940-41. Dad and Mother stayed close to the radio in the evenings, listening with sober faces to accounts of the bombing of Britain. A number of refugees came to live in the neighborhood—big-eyed, quiet children who were instinctively friendly to dogs. They talked to Skippy in the polite, clipped speech of England, and he gave them an affectionate Yankee welcome.

Very little of the news seemed to be good in those days. Americans were slowly waking up to the fact of danger—beginning to sense the crushing power of the *Luftwaffe* and the panzer divisions. People were studying the map of Europe and rubbing their eyes. The Selective Service law had been passed and the nation was starting to train an Army.

In June came Jane's college graduation, and Skip was left at home with Steve, while the rest of the family went out to Indiana to witness the event.

One night a few weeks later, Steve came home from his job and sat in the big living-room chair, holding Skippy in

Skippy's Family

his arms. He didn't say anything at first, but the old dog heard him clear his throat once or twice. Then he spoke to Dad.

"Don't believe I'll wait to be drafted," he said matter-of-factly. "When the time comes I'd rather do my fighting in the air. Always wanted to learn something about airplanes anyway."

Before the family went to Pocono in July, Steve had enlisted as a private in the Army Air Corps. He was stationed in Georgia at first, but in September he was sent to an air mechanic school in northern New Jersey, and was able to get home on short leaves fairly often.

Those were joyful occasions for Skip. With Beef away at college and playing football every week end, the little dog missed the boys' companionship. He began to prance and bark the moment he heard Steve's footstep on the walk, and he was even cured of a lifelong distaste for uniforms, now that one of his idols was wearing khaki.

It was on a Sunday early in December that something strangely disturbing shattered the tranquillity of the household. Both the boys were at home that day but Mother and Dad had gone to a housewarming some distance out in the country. Jane and Peg had gotten the dinner for their brothers, the dishes were done, and they were listening to the kind of orchestra music that always made Skip feel sleepy. Stretched out on a rug in the sun porch he was drowsing and toasting his old bones.

Skippy's Family

Suddenly the music was cut off and an excited voice began to speak. The words meant nothing to Skippy but the tone brought him to his feet, a whispered growl in his throat. Peggy Lu dropped her book on the floor and Beef gave a long, low whistle. Steve came quickly from the living room and Jane raced down the stairs.

"Did you hear what I heard?" . . . "Pearl Harbor!" . . . "We're at war!"

So it was in millions of homes across America. But Skip didn't know that. All he knew was that his family was upset. Steve's pass wasn't up till midnight but he went upstairs at once to pack his kitbag. Before he left, Dad and Mother rolled into the yard, and it was plain from their faces that they too had heard the news.

From that moment there was a change in the atmosphere of the household, and the old dog was deeply aware of it. Fear and worry had given way to a kind of tingling aliveness. He could feel it in Dad's quickened step as he came from the bus, and in the flutter of the big flag that hung above the door.

Within a month Dad was going out at queer times of day or night, dressed like an eskimo, to take his turn at the air spotters' post. If there was less laughter in the house now, it was because all were busier and their work had a purpose.

In February, Steve was graduated as an air mechanic, passed his exams for Aviation Cadet training and became engaged—all within a few days. Skip had already appraised the

Skippy's Family

bride-to-be and accepted her wholeheartedly. As far as he was concerned "Teddy" could be a full-fledged member of the family as soon as she liked.

The next two months turned out to be a hard and gloomy time. Bitter war news was coming from Bataan and Corregidor. But in the meantime other troubles struck closer home. Jane had an appendix operation that was followed by dangerous complications. There were blood transfusions and sleepless nights for the family. In all she remained in the hospital for six weeks. Mother was with her most of every day and Dad and Peggy Lu visited her often in the evenings. So old Skip stayed at home alone, wandering restlessly through the silent house. On Mother's return each day he was waiting, worried affection in his big, sad eyes. And when at last Jane came home, he kept special guard in her room, lying on the rug beside her bed until she was up and about once more.

The warm nights of spring found the family adjusted to a new kind of life, in which the central fact was war. Skippy raised his eyebrows at some of the queer goings-on. The ways of humans were surely unaccountable. What, for instance, were those pails of sand doing on the stairways? And why did Dad rush around closing shutters and turning off lights when those weird, howling noises came in the evening? The pitchy blackness of the house on such nights irked the old dog. Grumbling, he went off to his bed at the first wailing blast of the siren.

Skippy's Family

All vacation plans had to be revised that year. Beef was starting his senior year at college in June, on the new accelerated schedule. Mother and Dad and the girls thought longingly of Pocono, but gasoline rationing kept them at home through July. For the month of August they rented

a cottage at a quiet resort on the South Jersey coast, where Dad could commute by train. The location was a pleasant one. The back porch overlooked the Yacht Club Basin, and there were red sunsets above the bay and the marshes, where wheeling gulls cried plaintively. Morning and evening the tide made restful, lapping noises along the piling.

The seashore was a new experience for Skippy and he did not wholly approve of it. The water had a strange, rank smell, very different from his beloved lake. Five minutes after his arrival he went down on the rickety dock for a

Skippy's Family

drink, but one taste sent him hurrying back to dry land, nose wrinkled in disgust.

There were no cool-shadowed woods, no moss or ferns or deer. Instead he found a great deal of hot sand and thickets of bayberry so dense that he could hardly wriggle through them. Rabbits were there in abundance, but they kept safe in the brush, well out of his reach.

So the old dog moped around the yard or lay on the screened porch watching the gulls. He was homesick.

Dad, who was taking a two weeks' vacation, came back from the beach one afternoon, sunburned and hungry. When he had dressed and hung out his bathing trunks he came nosing into the kitchen.

"When do we eat?" he asked Mother.

"Suppertime," she told him firmly, "is in fifteen minutes. If you want something to do, fix up Skippy's bowl and call him."

Dad mixed the dehydrated dog food with water. "Here, Skip," he called. "Supper! Come on, boy!"

He went through the dining room and the living room and whistled up the stairs. "Must be outside," he said.

But all his calling produced no dog. The evening meal was eaten, the dishes washed. It was late that night before anybody remembered Skippy's absence. Dad called and whistled again, then went to bed. He was more annoyed than worried. There had been other occasions over the years when Skip went off gallivanting for a night. But he always came back

Skippy's Family

next day, sheepish and bleary-eyed.

The following morning they fully expected to find a contrite dog waiting on the doorstep. He wasn't there, nor did he put in an appearance during the day.

The street in front of the cottage was the island's main north-and-south thoroughfare. The traffic was fairly heavy in spite of wartime restrictions, and at night cars and trucks ran with parking lights only, for the blackout was maintained all along the shore. Every time Dad thought about Skippy, the sound of those passing vehicles made him wince. It wouldn't be easy, he knew, for a driver to see a small brown dog in the darkness.

He said nothing about it, for he didn't want to upset the girls, but he knew Mother was thinking the same thing. That evening he walked a long distance up and down the highway without finding any trace of Skip.

When he came home he found Peggy Lu crying quietly in a corner of the porch.

"Hold on, now, darling," he said. "What's the matter?"

"We shouldn't have let him go off alone," she sobbed. "He's so old."

"Old?" said Dad. "Sure he's old, but he can take care of himself."

"He isn't like he used to be, Daddy. He's deaf, and he can't see as well—and he's slow. I'm afraid he—he couldn't get out of the way, if a car was coming."

"Oh, shucks," said her father, trying to be reassuring.

Skippy's Family

"He'll be back."

But his own faith was very low when he went to bed. Was it possible that he had refused to notice those signs of advancing years in the old dog? He thought back over the past few weeks and knew Peg was right. He had taken Skippy's ability to adjust himself to a new environment too much for granted, and had paid very little attention to his comings and goings.

There was a violent thunderstorm that night, but it failed to drive away the heat. The next day was sultry, with a blazing sun and a land breeze. Nobody in the family was either cheerful or talkative. To all of them had come the final realization that it was no longer any use hoping for Skippy's return.

On the beach, after their morning swim, Jane stretched her brown legs and looked at the sea. "I guess we're going to miss him," she said. "He was an awful pest sometimes, but he loved us."

"Yes," said Peg. "Remember how he used to take us to school when we were little?"

"And how we dressed him up in doll clothes?" Jane replied.

"And how he used to defend me when he slept in my room?" Mother put in. "I'll never forget that night when you came home late, Pink, and tiptoed in to tell me about the party. Skip didn't even growl. He just grabbed you by the ankle, ready to bite if you laid a hand on me."

Skippy's Family

"Some watchdog!" Dad smiled. "He never even woke up when that prowler broke in through the sun porch last spring and stole the bananas!"

"He was a wonderful watchdog," protested Peg, close to tears. "I'll bet he chased away plenty of burglars when he was young and his ears were sharp."

There were so many incidents to remember in the little dog's long life that they sat there for another hour, easing their hearts by talking about him. Then gradually they lapsed into silence again.

Toward the end of that afternoon, Mother discovered that there was only a tiny piece of ice left in the refrigerator.

"That hopeless idiot of an iceman," she complained to Dad, "has gone by again without looking at the sign. I'm afraid you'll have to go and get some ice if we don't want the food to spoil."

Grumbling, Dad left his porch chair and went out to the car. The ice plant was a mile up the island. He drove north along the hot, white highway and turned in on a side street. With the fifty-pound chunk of ice on newspapers in the car, he pulled out again to the main road, pausing at the stop sign. Down the avenue there were no cars in sight. Up the road—he looked again, squinting against the sun.

A quarter of a mile away, in the middle of the broad concrete, there was a brownish dot that did not move.

Dad swung the car north and drove toward the small object. As he drew nearer he could see it was a dog, and he

Skippy's Family

grew surer with each second that the dog was Skippy.

Yet at the last moment, when he stopped the car on the roadside, he was no longer sure. The little animal stood forlornly in the heat and glare, swaying on its feet, head and tail drooping, eyes half closed. Water dripped from its muddy, matted coat and its body was pitifully gaunt.

Dad got out and went toward the dog. "Skipper?" he said gently. "What's the matter, boy?"

Yes, it was Skippy. He tried to turn toward the voice, staggered and slumped in a heap on the road. Dad picked up the limp little body and laid it on the seat of the car. Then he made for home as fast as he could drive.

The bundle of bones and wet fur that he brought into the kitchen seemed to be lifeless. Only the faintest movement of the ribs showed that Skip was still breathing. They tried to tempt him with food and water but he still lay there in a coma, his eyes filmed with exhaustion and pain.

At last, just before bedtime, the little dog lapped a few drops of water from the pan when Peg lifted his head.

"I don't know whether he'll live through the night," said Dad. "But there isn't much more we can do. At least, he's home. He's back with us again."

TWELVE

As usual, Mother was the first one up. She slipped into a kimono and tiptoed down to the kitchen. Skippy lay just as they had left him but his body twitched a little when she approached, and he looked up at her with a gleam of consciousness in his eyes.

She stroked his head, murmuring words of encouragement. And when the pan of water was moved close he succeeded in drinking a little without help. Then, with a heroic effort, he got his front paws under him and tried to rise. It was no use. His hind legs still lay sprawled and helpless.

"Paralyzed!" said Dad, when he saw the dog. "But he was standing up yesterday when I found him, so I don't see how his back can be broken. Here, old poochie, let me feel your spine. No—there's no break there."

After breakfast they debated taking Skippy over to the mainland and trying to locate a veterinarian. But while they talked there came a scrabbling sound from the kitchen. By some miracle of will the gritty old dog had managed to get to his feet. A cheer went up from the whole family as he

Skippy's Family

stood there, lurching groggily.

From that moment Skippy began to recover. His progress seemed painfully slow at times, but they could see him get better from day to day. At first he had difficulty controlling his hind legs. He was like a baby learning to walk—falling down and gamely getting up again.

It had been his habit to sleep upstairs in the hall, as near the family as he could get. The second night after his return, they made a comfortable place for him in the kitchen and went up to bed. Half an hour later, Mother was roused from her first sleep by a plaintive whimpering. She rose and went to the head of the stairs. Part of the way up was Skippy. He had started to climb and somehow dragged himself to the fifth step where his strength finally gave out. Mother carried him the rest of the way and he lay down contentedly outside her door.

Often, during those weeks of his convalescence, the family speculated on what had happened to the little dog. There were several theories. Based on the evidence at hand, Dad believed Skippy had been hit by a car or a truck the first night and tossed to the side of the road, where he had lain, unable to move. After a day and a night of helplessness he had recovered enough to crawl across to the bay shore. There, in an effort to quench his thirst, he had fallen in. That would account for the dripping state in which Dad had found him.

Peggy Lu had a different idea. Skip had been very home-

Skippy's Family

sick, she explained. The evening he disappeared he had set out with a vague idea of leaving the seashore and finding his way home. Perhaps he had actually crossed one of the bridges and started north along the main shore road. Then, she suggested, the thunderstorm had frightened him.

"You know how he always crawled under Daddy's bed when there were loud claps of thunder?" she reminded them. "I think he wanted to come back and lost his way in the storm. Perhaps he got out on the marsh. There was the bay in front of him and he jumped in and tried to swim across to the island. My idea is he was just about drowned when he finally got to this side—and so tired his hind legs wouldn't work any more. It was pure luck that when he pulled himself up on the road Dad saw him before a car came along and hit him."

Jane leaned down and pulled the old dog's ears. "If only you could talk," she said, "we'd know the whole story, wouldn't we, Skip? But I'm afraid you'll never tell us."

By Labor Day, when the family left the seashore, Skip no longer needed help in getting up and down steps. His stiffness was still apparent for a week or two after he got home, but he improved steadily. The first day among familiar surroundings brought back his zest for living. He spent hours in a luxurious tour of all his neighborhood haunts. When he came back his tail was waving gaily above his back and his face wore a look of satisfaction that had not been there since he first went to the shore.

Skippy's Family

He was well enough, that fall, to share the household's mounting excitement as Beef's football team swept through game after game on its way to an all-victorious season. Calling it "Beef's team" really meant something that year, for

he was captain. The family had season tickets, and all of them sat in the stands bursting with pride when the boy trotted on the field at the head of his squad. Dad cheered himself hoarse and Mother watched, pale and silent, till the scrimmage unpiled itself after each play.

They seriously discussed taking Skippy to one of the games, but decided against it. There were already several dogs too many straying out on the gridiron, and Skip would have been unhappy locked in the car.

Skippy's Family

He could understand the fact that John was a hero, however. Hadn't he always known it? Sometimes the family brought the burly youngster home after a game and Skippy lay blissfully in his arms, lifting his nose now and then to

lick the cuts and contusions that always decorated his adored one's face.

Beef's graduation was in January. For a few happy weeks the old dog enjoyed the boy's daily company while he awaited Army orders to start Aviation Cadet training. Then in February Skip was left at a boarding kennel while the whole family went to South Carolina for Steve's wedding. With their return, and Beef's departure, life settled down

Skippy's Family

once more into its quiet routine.

Wisely, the little dog had given up his long journeys around the town. He contented himself now with a much smaller radius of operations. It included the home grounds, the orchard across the street, and perhaps a dozen neighboring yards. But while his world had shrunk, he seemed to get as much pleasure from it as ever. Trotting purposefully from one point of interest to the next, he might have been a faithful old watchman making his rounds.

When the snow disappeared and the lawn began to grow green in the spring, the late afternoon usually found Skip lying out on the terrace, waiting for Dad's return from work. He didn't race out to meet him now, as he had once done. At the sound of footsteps he would get up, give a questioning bark or two, and wait uncertainly till Dad was within a few yards of him. Then his greeting was as warm as it had always been.

It was the family doctor who finally diagnosed the cause of this change in Skippy. He had stopped in one evening to see Peggy, who was recovering from a spring cold. In the hall he found the old dog waiting, as usual, to speed the parting guest.

"Hello there, Old-timer," said the doctor. He grinned, and stooped to pat Skip's grizzled head. Then he took him closer to the table lamp and sat down, looking into the little dog's face.

"How old is he?" he asked.

Skippy's Family

"We've had him fifteen years and a few months," Dad replied. "You'd never know it, would you, Doc?"

The doctor nodded thoughtfully. "Say sixteen years old," he said. "That would be about the equivalent of eighty in a man. Wouldn't you think an eighty-year-old was pretty remarkable if he didn't have to wear glasses?"

He lifted the dog's head and beckoned Dad nearer. "See those eyes?" he said. "You wouldn't notice it, but there's just the beginning of a cataract. Poor old chap, he's starting to go blind."

To Dad, Skippy's eyes looked as limpid and trusting and expressive as ever, but he knew the doctor must be right. It was something that must be expected in aging dogs, and it explained some of the differences he had noticed in Skip's behavior. Almost certainly it would account for the old fellow's avoidance of Main Street traffic, and his hesitation about recognizing friends until they came within smelling distance.

In many ways that summer of 1943 was among the most peaceful and pleasant that Skip had ever known. True, he missed the boys, but the rest of the family stayed right at home. Dad had a victory garden back of the garage, where he sweated away at spading and planting, hoeing and weeding. A failure in most respects, the little patch produced extraordinary quantities of string beans and tomatoes, and Mother and the girls spent hectic days canning them.

From the morning in April when a wagonload of manure

Skippy's Family

was delivered, to the harvesting of the final tomato in September, Skippy took a special interest in that garden.

Dad had a theory that the old dog simply enjoyed watch-

ing other people work. He had always stayed close to Dad when he cut the grass, flopping down happily in the exact path of the lawn mower as it made each round, and waiting till it was almost upon him before he moved. Now he enter-

Skippy's Family

tained himself for hours with the spectacle of Dad's labors in the garden. He sniffed curiously at each fresh-turned clod of earth and shared with his sore-muscled master the thrill of seeing each tiny green sprout thrust its head above the ground. He learned from harsh experience not to leave his footprints in the seedbeds.

On hot Saturdays in July he lolled in the refreshing shade between the cornstalks and listened drowsily to the clink of Dad's hoe in the next row. But the best times of all were those exciting occasions when the vegetables were gathered—the scarlet radishes, the slim green beans and the golden carrots—lovingly placed in the basket by Dad's earth-grimed fingers.

With the approach of fall, Peggy Lu's trunk was packed and the last of the children set forth for college. Skippy hardly had time to miss her, for at 1:30 the next morning Steve and Teddy drove into the yard. Out of the car with their luggage tumbled a taffy-colored cocker pup. Her name, it appeared, was Candy, and for two days she turned the place upside down. With the nervous energy of a small tornado she combined the most fetching feminine wiles and graces.

Skippy was entranced. He tried to keep up with her in a frantic game of tag all around the house, and when his breath was gone he lay panting and submissive while she chewed at his ears. At last, so weary he could hardly stagger, the old dog broke away from his little tormentor and made his way

Skippy's Family

to Mother with a mute appeal for help.

When Candy had gone off to Georgia with the lieutenant and his bride, tranquillity returned to the household. At least it was tranquil for Skippy, who slept most of the day following their departure. But something happened that week that was disturbing to Dad.

At a meeting of the town's local governing body a new dog ordinance had passed its first reading. Backed by a group of irate victory gardeners and a scattering of citizens who simply disliked animals, it proposed stiff penalties for any owner who permitted his dog to leave his own property except on a six-foot leash. This regulation was to apply throughout the months from April to November of each year. And for purposes of enforcement it was further provided that a full-time policeman be appointed as dogcatcher at once.

Apparently the backers of the ordinance had moved in fast and impressed the Township Committee by weight of argument before any opposition could be organized. Now the news was spreading and indignant dog owners were ready to rise in their wrath.

Dad talked to some of the neighbors. There was to be an open meeting of the Township Committee at which objections could be offered. Perhaps there was still a chance of doing something about the ordinance. That evening Dad sat down with his pad and pencil, and while Skippy dozed on the rug at his feet, he composed a letter.

THIRTEEN

THE local weekly paper reached its readers on Thursday. By that time the dog law had become a burning issue in the town, and took up a large share of the news section. Prominent on the front page was Dad's message:

"To the Editor
"Dear Sir:
"This is a letter about Skippy. It would be more fitting if he could write it himself, but though he is 16 years old and of reasonable intelligence, he has never learned to read or write.

"Skippy came to us about a week before Christmas, in 1927. It was a disagreeable night, bleak and blowy, with slushy snow on the ground. He had been hurt, possibly struck by a car. He dragged himself up on our front steps and huddled there by the door. When I came home, half an hour later, he was a member of the family.

Skippy's Family

"I took one look at the collarless, bedraggled little mongrel and decided firmly that he should be taken away and put out of his misery. But as often happens in such cases I was overruled. The children were tearful or rebellious, according to age and sex, and they found an unexpected ally in their mother. 'Let's keep him till tomorrow and see if he's better,' she urged.

"By the next night I knew I was beaten. Skippy had been tenderly washed and brushed. His tail was a gay plume and his eyes would have melted a much stonier heart than mine. He had found people he could love and trust.

"Through all the years since then, Skippy has been our faithful playmate, companion and guardian. For all his doubtful ancestry and diminutive size he has always been a gentleman, always valiant. I have seen him tackle strange dogs three times his weight and run them off the premises.

"When the younger children started school he went with them each day and escorted them home. When the family went on vacations to the Poconos or the shore, he went too, keeping a watchful eye on our belongings.

"In his younger days he roamed over a considerable part of the town, visiting friends and checking up on the latest news of dogdom, as announced at various canine post offices. The last year or two he has grown somewhat stiff with age, and neither his sight nor his hearing is as keen as it used to be. His range of travel has narrowed to a few hundred yards

Skippy's Family

from the house. But he still likes to be out by himself in the sun and the air, minding his own affairs with all his old, sturdy independence.

"Twice this summer I have seen him bury some treasure in a corner of our victory garden, and on one occasion a sprouting bean vine was destroyed. Otherwise he has taken a deep interest in the gardening work, watching me for hours while I dug and planted, weeded and harvested.

"Now comes the news of an extraordinarily harsh dog ordinance. I haven't told Skippy about it, and I hope I shall never have to. Those who demanded such a law must surely have slight understanding of dogs. I am told the measure was prompted by the complaints of a relatively small number of local gardeners.

"In my own immediate neighborhood there are six flourishing victory gardens and six dogs. To the best of my knowledge they have spent the summer in complete harmony. An occasional stray dog wanders through, sniffs at a garbage pail or two and goes his way. We don't encourage such visits but we don't especially resent them.

"Dogs are not vegetarians. They have no taste for raw vegetables or growing plants. If they dig in tilled earth it is to bury one of the rare bones they can find in these rationed days. And they do it for the same prudent reason that makes a man work in his garden—to provide against a future time of scarcity. At a conservative estimate I would say the total

damage done to gardens by dogs would amount to less than one-fifth of that done by rabbits—so carefully safeguarded in their freedoms by law.

"No, I don't want to put Skippy on a six-foot leash. After so many happy years he wouldn't understand. I think it would break his heart.

"If this community's 1100 dog owners feel the same way, the Township Committee offers them an opportunity to say so next Monday night. We have had a

Skippy's Family

reasonable and sensible dog law. Is there any justifiable cause for changing it to a cruel one?

"In behalf of all decent dog citizens . . ."

The letter was signed with Dad's name.

* * *

Over the week end the town buzzed with discussion. When Dad got to the Town Hall that Monday evening he found the committee room packed with people and overflowing on the stairs. With the crowd still gathering it was decided that the meeting should be moved to the big gymnasium in the Community House, a block away.

That was an occasion to be remembered. The discussion was orderly enough, but it was obvious from the beginning that feeling ran high. One after another, some twenty people spoke from various parts of the hall. Nearly all were dog lovers, bitterly attacking the ordinance. For the defense, not more than two appeared, and their efforts were half-hearted. One touch of comedy lightened the serious tone of the meeting when a long-suffering postman rose and plaintively asked for an amendment to the law. His trousers had been torn by a dog some years before and he hoped the ordinance would specify their replacement at the town's expense.

The Township Committeemen sat through it all, red-faced and uncomfortable. At last the Chairman got up in an attempt to justify their action, but before he had time to state his case the night was rent by the scream of air raid sirens. The meeting broke up in haste. Everybody rushed

Skippy's Family

off, trying to get home before the "Red" warning signal and the blackout.

Some of the more cynical members of the community suspected afterward that the sudden air raid drill was a trick, arranged to get the Committee out of an embarrassing position. But in any case the meeting had cleared the atmosphere.

Dad came home with the jubilant feeling that Skippy's letter had done some good after all. The following week it was announced that, though the ordinance would remain on the books, its interpretation would be made as liberal as possible.

Skippy must have been puzzled at the amount of petting he received in the next few days. If he stirred from the home yard an admiring neighbor was sure to point him out to passersby.

"That's Skippy," he would announce. "That's the dog that was in the letter to the paper. Yep, he's what I call a good citizen."

Overnight the little dog had become famous from one end of the town to the other. It was undoubtedly a surprise to him to find he had so many new friends all at once.

As far as he was concerned the ordinance might as well never have been heard of. He pursued the even course of his daily life without restraints. Since he never roved very far now, the police never picked him up. And if they had, it is likely that the name on his collar would have served as a passport.

Cold weather followed the heavy rains of fall. The family

Skippy's Family

shivered in sweaters, for the house was kept at a temperature of 65 to save rationed fuel. Skip didn't mind the cold. His coat was as thick and warm as ever. But it was noticeable that his movements were slowed up on damp days. Mother worried about the old dog's increasing stiffness.

"I think he has rheumatism," she told Dad. "Sometimes when he moves on his pillow at night I hear him whine as if it hurt him."

They tried giving him vitamin capsules but he succeeded in spitting most of them out. Those he did swallow had no apparent effect on his aching joints.

On clear, dry days he spruced up and trotted about as gaily as ever. One bright December morning when Dad went out to shovel the walks after a snowfall he found Skip racing around the yard and rolling in the powdery drifts with as much pleasure as a two-year-old.

They had a lonesome Christmas that year—the first they had had to celebrate without either of the boys. Everything was done as usual—the tree—the lights and decorations—the wreaths in the windows—even the stockings. But when all was finished that Christmas Eve, Skip found Peggy Lu standing alone in front of the hearth in the living room. She looked at the pitifully short row of stockings and dabbed at her eyes with a moist handkerchief. Troubled, the old dog reared up on his hind legs and licked her hand. He understood how she felt. In his own way he was doing his best to comfort her.

FOURTEEN

SKIP seemed closer to the family that winter than ever before. It was partly because he spent more of his time indoors, partly because the circle of the household was drawn tighter by the absence of the boys and Peg. But in addition Mother and Dad gave the old fellow more attention. They could see him aging little by little. His appetite, always good in his younger days, began to desert him, and he had to be tempted by tidbits left over from the table —scraps of tender meat or fish, muffins and other dainties.

The gray film over his eyes had become more noticeable. Knowing every inch of the house and yard by heart, he still trotted about as usual, but once or twice he betrayed his blindness by running into a door that he didn't know was closed. Several times, while foraging in the shrubbery in front of the house, he fell into one of the cellar window wells and stayed there whimpering until Dad found him and lifted him out.

His ears, once so keen, were failing him, too. Even the ringing of the doorbell sometimes went unheard when he

Skippy's Family

was taking a nap. That was hard for Dad and Mother to believe, for Skip had always dashed to the door at the sound of a car stopping or a footstep on the walk.

In March Dad went off on a long business trip to the Pacific Coast. When he came home there was no Skippy in the hall to welcome him.

"Where's Skip?" he asked, after the greetings were over.

Mother looked sad. "He's been lying on his pillow in the chair all day," she said. "Poor old thing—he's been so crippled with rheumatism he could hardly move."

Dad went in and patted the old dog's gray head. "Whatsamatter, boy?" he asked gently.

Skippy opened his dim eyes and nuzzled at Dad's hand. When he tried to get up he fell off the chair to the floor with a painful thump. Shocked, Dad picked him up and held him in his arms.

"What are we going to do about him?" he asked Mother.

She shook her head. "I talked to the veterinarian yesterday," she said. "He says at Skip's age he can't do anything to help. It will probably get worse as time goes on."

The next day was warm and sunny and the little dog was definitely more comfortable. He limped around the yard, ate a little, and found a soft place on the rug in the sun porch, where he dozed for hours. Dad heaved a sigh of relief and put off the decision he knew he would have to make sooner or later.

For a whole month Skip seemed to be reasonably well.

Skippy's Family

He was very thin and he walked stiffly but he made no complaint. As the warm weather continued, Dad began to plan his garden. The day he turned the first spadeful of earth Skippy was there beside him, and the dog continued to supervise the job until all the early seeds were in.

Then, early in May, it turned chilly again. Rain fell all one dreary Saturday and by evening Skip was in the grip of his old enemy. Dad tried to make a comfortable bed for him with a pillow on the floor, but he would have none of it. Blindly he tried to climb into the familiar chair only to topple back in pain and weakness. Dad was afraid the dog would fall if he slept there but to humor him he replaced the pillow in its accustomed place and lifted Skippy up.

When he tiptoed out of the room his face was bleak. "It's more than I can stand," he told Mother. "Every breath hurts him. And when he tried to turn around in his bed before he lay down and couldn't make it—gosh—it almost broke me down."

All night they could hear Skippy moaning softly at intervals. He was no better in the morning, and the family had very little appetite for breakfast. When the table was cleared, Dad looked at Mother with a question.

She was silent for a moment. "He shouldn't have to suffer any more," she said at last. "But I can't say it."

Dad went to the telephone and called the vet. After he hung up he came out to the kitchen. "Doc'll be ready in half an hour," he told Jane quietly. "Soon as the dishes are

Skippy's Family

done we'll take him up there."

There was a song sparrow singing in the mild spring rain as Dad carried Skip out to the car. Jane got in behind the wheel and drove down the lane between lilac bushes and dogwood trees in bloom. Half a mile up Main Street they entered the vet's driveway.

The kindly man was waiting at the door of his office. He understood Dad's unhappiness. "It's all right," he said, taking Skippy gently in his arms. "You're doing the right thing."

"Will he—" Dad tried to ask.

"No," the vet reassured him. "He'll just go quietly to sleep. You can come in if you like."

Dad shook his head miserably. "I'll wait out here. So long, Skip." He turned away quickly and went to sit in the car.

The rain pattered softly on the roof and Dad and Jane sat in silence for a little while. Then the girl began to speak.

"It's such a lovely time of year," she said. "Those lilacs. I don't suppose I'll ever forget how sweet they smelled this morning. Poor old pooch—he always loved the spring."

They talked quietly, remembering happier times when

Skippy's Family

Skip was young. And little by little Dad felt the weight lifting from his heart.

When the vet came out he was carrying a neatly wrapped bundle that Dad placed tenderly on the back seat. "A great little dog," the man said. "I know how you feel. But he's done with pain now. He's at peace."

Dad nodded, not feeling like speaking just then. As they drove home, Jane mentioned something that had been on her mind.

"The boys will understand," she said, "but I don't think we'd better tell Peg till she gets home from college. She's starting her exams this week and it might be pretty tough for her. Just think—she was only a baby when Skip came and she's never known the time that he wasn't one of us."

Dad believed he knew where Skippy would want to lie. It was a corner of the back yard where the two hedges made a sort of sheltered arbor and the sun fell in the afternoon. There he dug the grave deep, laying the green sods carefully aside. Once, as he worked, the spade clinked on something hard, and he turned up an old, gray beef bone, buried there long ago. He took an odd comfort from putting it back where he had found it.

Mother and Jane stood by while Dad lowered the little bundle to its final resting place. When the turf had been put back, he shaped and painted a small white marker. On it was printed in simple letters: SKIPPY, 1927-1944.

* * *

Skippy's Family

Some time, no doubt, the family will have a dog again. More than one well-meaning friend has urged Dad and Mother to get one as the only sensible course. The children are agreed that it would be nice to have a pup around the place, and Steve and Teddy have generously offered the pick of Candy's first litter.

But there will never be another Skippy.

www.ingramcontent.com/pod-product-compliance
Lightning Source LLC
Chambersburg PA
CBHW030524080526
44586CB00011B/312